chickensalad

by barbara lauterbach :: photographs by sheri giblin

# chickensalad

fifty favorite recipes

CHRONICLE BOOKS

SAN FRANCISCO

Library of Congress Cataloging-
in-Publication Data available.

ISBN 0-8118-3712-2

Manufactured in China

Food and Prop styling by
EK Food Productions:
Erin Quon and Kim Konecny
Photographer's assistant:
Guarina Lopez
Designed by Lesley Feldman
The photographer would also like
to thank Patte McDowell
*"for use of a beautiful location"*

Distributed in Canada
by Raincoast Books
9050 Shaughnessy Street
Vancouver, British Columbia
V6P 6E5

10 9 8 7 6 5 4 3 2 1

Chronicle Books LLC
85 Second Street
San Francisco, California 94105

www.chroniclebooks.com

page 2: Poor Man's Lobster Roll
Salad, page 27

**permissions ::**

Chicken Salad Verde Anna Teresa
(page 32), adapted from *Menus
for Pasta* by Anna Teresa Callen,
Crown Publishers, New York,
copyright 1985. Used by permission of Anna Teresa Callen.

The Best Chicken Salad No
One Remembers Eating (page
63), adapted from *The Border
Cookbook* by Cheryl Alters
Jamison and Bill Jamison, Harvard
Common Press, Boston, copy-
right 1995. Used by permission
of Harvard Common Press.

Hay Day's Spicy Chicken Salad
(page 78), adapted from *The
Hay Day Cookbook* by Maggie
Stearns and Sallie Y. Williams,
Atheneum, New York, copyright
1986. Used by permission
of Alexander T. Van Rensselaer.

**acknowledgments ::**

Heartfelt thanks and deepest
gratitude to the many people
who made this book possible.

To Susan Ginsburg, my literary
agent, for her sharp intuitive-
ness and support.

To the group at Chronicle
Books, all of whom with
which it is a delight to work.

Bill LeBlond, editor extraordi-
naire, for excellent instinct
and guidance; Amy Treadwell,
for her knowledge of the process, keen eye, and gentle good
humor; Sheri Giblin, who has
done an incredible job of photo-
graphing a potentially mono-
chromatic subject and making it
leap from the pages; Azi Rad, an
art director with enormous
vision; Jan Hughes and Doug
Ogan for superb attention to
detail; Rebecca Pepper for copy-
editing in such a thorough yet
friendly fashion; Steve Kim for
the beautiful finished product;
and last but certainly not least,
both Michele Fuller and Christi
Cavallaro for their amazing
publicity and marketing efforts.
You are a fabulous team.

My sister Jo and her family, for
their contributions, and Aunt Jo
Atley for her memories of Maine.

Lora Brody, for once again
being the mentor of mentors.

The WWW walking group and
Cynthia Barnes for enthusiastic
testing and tasting and support.

Richard Lobb, of the National
Chicken Council, for providing
such useful information.

Without the love and support
of all of these people, this
book would not have happened.

## dedication

To Liz Lapham, my assistant, for her infinite common sense and ability to see the humorous side: a good coach, a good cook, and above all, a good friend.

To my children, C.H. and Lisa, and their spouses Lisa and Bill, for their many contributions and enthusiasm for their mother's endeavors.

To Tom Wilson, for his insight, wisdom, experience, patience, and above all for being there for me.

bacon, lettuce, and tomato chicken salad wrap :: page 55

# contents

# introduction

White gloves, pearls, and an air of elegance come to mind when I think of chicken salad. Long a favorite of ladies who lunch, the bland chicken salad of more tranquil times now takes center stage as an exciting and upbeat dish. Imagine a spicy Asian chicken salad, an elegant salad of chicken and crisp green sugar snap peas, or a crunchy, well-seasoned fried chicken salad. Whether held together by a silky mayonnaise or a flavorful vinaigrette, moist, tasty, plump morsels of chicken give the cook a palette upon which a variety of delicious ingredients can be blended.

Not only is chicken salad a universal favorite, it is also inexpensive, easy to prepare, and can, with very little effort, be made in large quantities for any number of people. The good news for today's busy, multitasking home cook is that many chicken salads improve when made several hours, if not a day, ahead.

As an experienced cooking teacher and chicken salad aficionado, I know that home cooks are always seeking dishes that look terrific and taste even better, but that are not too time-consuming to prepare. This book includes traditional recipes collected from family (Cacklebird Salad, page 22), from friends (Dottie's Mah-Jongg Chicken Salad , page 30), and from students in my cooking classes (Curried Chutney Chicken Salad, page 66), along with new and innovative recipes. It also contains salads made with other poultry (Smoked Turkey and Melon Salad with Citrus Mint Vinaigrette, page 94),

as well as hot salads (Chicken 'n' Chips Hot Salad, page 38), since chicken salad need not be served only in warm weather. The recipes illustrate the versatility of chicken salad, whether it is made with vegetables, fruits, rice, or pasta. Each recipe also includes suggestions for presenting and serving the salad.

To streamline the recipes, I've given master instructions for cooking poultry for salad. I've also included basic techniques for toasting nuts, making mayonnaise and vinaigrette, roasting peppers, and making croutons. In addition, you'll find safe handling tips and information on organic, kosher, and frozen poultry.

According to the National Chicken Council, Americans eat more than eighty pounds of chicken per person each year. It is my goal here to help you prepare salads featuring the nation's favorite bird as creatively as possible.

# thebasics

Many of the recipes in this book specify a master recipe for cooking chicken for that particular salad. There are several ways to prepare chicken for salad. You may roast an entire chicken or just the breasts or thighs, or you may poach a whole bird or the parts in seasoned liquids. Some people feel that roasting yields better flavor; others prefer the moister taste of a poached bird. The question of whether to use the whole bird or just the white meat of the breast is also a matter of taste. Some prefer a salad made with all white meat, while others insist that incorporating some dark meat intensifies the flavor. Some like their chicken finely chopped; others prefer a medium dice or more sizable chunks of the meat. Try the recipes both ways and make your personal choice. Of course, leftover cooked chicken is perfectly acceptable in most of these recipes. You will find a salad for every taste in this book.

If you don't have time to cook chicken in advance, the chicken that you purchase, already roasted, at the deli counter of your local supermarket is a wonderful time-saver in the preparation of chicken salad. Another option is to use canned chicken.

If you are using leftover cooked chicken or other poultry, cut up the required amount for the recipe. (See "Chicken Meat Yields" below.) It is not necessary to recook leftover chicken.

# masterrecipesforcooking chickenforsalad

**chicken meat yields ::**

: The average broiler/fryer weighs between 2¼ and 4 pounds.

: A 3-pound chicken, roasted, yields 4 to 4½ cups chicken meat, both white and dark.

: Chicken breasts vary greatly in size. A whole breast (2 half breasts, attached), skinned and boned, weighing anywhere from 10 to 14 ounces, will yield 2 to 2½ cups chicken meat.

: One pound of deli rotisserie chicken or turkey breast yields 3 cups diced meat.

: One 5-ounce can of chicken yields ½ cup meat.

: Five chicken thighs, skinned and boned, weighs about 1 pound and will yield 2½ to 3 cups of dark meat.

**types of chicken ::**

Here are the primary sizes and types of chicken available in the supermarket.

: **broiler chicken**
   Raised for meat products, 2½ to 4 pounds. Use: Broiling or grilling.

: **broiler roaster**
   5 to 6 pounds. Use: Broiling or grilling, split, or roasting.

: **cornish game hen**
Usually about 2 pounds. Use: Broiling
or grilling, split, or roasting.

: **heavy young broiler roaster**
6 to 8 pounds, sold fresh or frozen.
Use: Primarily roasting.

: **capon**
Surgically desexed male broiler, weighing
7 to 9 pounds. Use: Primarily roasting.

: **heavy hen**
Breeder hen no longer productive
for laying eggs, usually 5 to 5½ pounds.
Use: Soups, stews, or casseroles.

**"nuggets" of chicken information ::**

This list clarifying some of the terms used
to describe chicken was provided by Richard
Lobb of the National Chicken Council.

: **hormone free**
Any meat or chicken in the United States could
be labeled hormone-free, as the U.S. goverment
does not allow the use of artificial or added
hormones. Steroids are also banned. The term
is for the most part a marketing concept.

: **free range**
There is no official federal government defini-
tion of free-range chickens. It implies chickens
foraging outdoors where they will, but in real-
ity they stay close to their water and feed, which
are generally in the chicken house. The U.S.

Department of Agriculture (USDA) permits the
term to be used if the chickens have access to
an area outside the chicken house for some
part of the day. However, an article in *Consumer
Reports* magazine quoted a "free range" pro-
ducer who stated that "It's not in the chickens'
nature that if you give them a 15-acre pasture
they're going to gallop and jump and roll over."
In blind taste tests, conventionally raised
chickens were found to be comparable to the
free-range ones.

: **natural**
The USDA permits this label when a chicken
has no additives and only minimal processing.

: **organic**
This label varies according to state regulations;
there is no federal standard. The use of the word
"organic" indicates that no artificial pesticides
or manufactured fertilizers were used, so an
organically grown chicken would have to be fed
organically grown feed and not be medicated in
anyway.

: **kosher**
A chicken bearing a kosher label indicates
the chicken has been produced and processed
under rabbinical supervision according to
Jewish dietary laws. The slaughter is carried out
by hand, and the carcasses are soaked in salted
water to bring out residual blood.

**safety tips for handling chicken ::**

: After purchasing chicken, be sure to refrigerate
it as soon as possible. Store it in the coldest
part of the refrigerator, or freeze it if you won't
be using it within two days. You can keep it in
the freezer, well wrapped, for up to six months.

: Thaw frozen chicken only in the refrigerator
(allow up to 24 hours) or in cold water. To
do this, place chicken, in its original wrap, in
cold water, changing the water often. It
should take about 2 hours to thaw using this
method. Chicken parts may also be thawed
in a microwave, using the microwave manufac-
turer's instructions for thawing.

: Be sure to wash hands, knives, and cutting
boards with detergent after preparing raw
chicken, before they are used to prepare any
other foods.

: Chicken should always be cooked until well
done. A meat thermometer should register
180°F for a whole bird, 180°F for dark bone-
in parts (thighs, wings, and drumsticks), 170°F
for white bone-in parts, and 160°F for boneless parts.

: To check for doneness, use a fork to pierce
the chicken. The juices should run clear. If they
are pink, the chicken isn't done.

: Cooked, cut-up chicken should be consumed
within two days.

13

# master recipe for poaching chicken for salad

When chicken is poached in a liquid for salad, the result is tender and juicy meat. Both white and dark meat respond well to poaching. The liquid used is important. If it is not seasoned properly, the chicken will have a bland, boiled taste. This method works for either a whole chicken or for chicken parts, such as breasts and thighs. The following directions are for two whole bone-in, skin-on chicken breasts and will yield 4½ to 5 cups of meat, enough for most recipes in this book. The bones and skin are included for flavor, but you can poach boneless, skinless breasts or thighs in the same manner. Adjust the liquid to the amount of chicken you are using. Bring the water just to a rolling boil, but do not continue boiling or the meat will be tough.

**yields 4½ to 5 cups of poached chicken ::**

: 2 whole chicken breasts, skin-on and bone-in

: Chicken stock or water to cover by 1 inch

: ¼ cup white wine or vermouth

: 3 or 4 sprigs flat-leaf parsley

: 1 onion, sliced

: 1 stalk celery with leaves, broken into pieces

: Salt and freshly ground black pepper

**preparation ::**

Place the chicken breasts in a large 3- to 4-quart saucepan. Add the stock or water, wine or vermouth, parsley, onion, and celery. Add a dash of salt and pepper.

Bring to a boil, and then turn off the heat but leave the pan on the burner. Cover the pan and let the contents cool for about 25 minutes. If the breasts are very large, the time will be longer. When done, the meat will be firm to the touch and should register around 160°F on a meat thermometer. If you cut into it, there should be no pink flesh.

If you are poaching a whole chicken, the method is the same. However, when the stock or water reaches the boiling point, reduce the heat and simmer the chicken for 10 minutes before turning off the heat. Cover the pan and let cool for about 25 minutes.

Remove the chicken from the liquid, strip off the skin, and pull the meat from the bones. Remove any visible fat. Proceed with the recipe. Strain and reserve the stock for soups or for more poaching, if you are poaching several batches of chicken. It will become richer each time you use it. The stock will keep, covered, in the refrigerator for 2 days or can be frozen for up to 3 months.

# masterrecipe for roasting chickenforsalad

When chicken is roasted with the skin on, the flavor of the fat permeates the meat and contributes to a delicious taste. You may roast chicken parts, such as breasts, thighs, or drumsticks, or a whole chicken.

## roast chicken parts

: Chicken parts of your choice
: Salt and freshly ground black pepper
: Softened butter

**preparation ::**

Preheat the oven to 400°F. Line a baking sheet with foil.

Rinse the chicken parts and pat them dry with paper towels. Season lightly with salt and pepper and rub all over with softened butter. Place the parts on the baking sheet.

Roast the parts for 35 to 45 minutes, basting them with the drippings in the pan several times. Dark meat will take longer than white meat.

If using a meat thermometer, the temperature should be 170°F, and the juices should run clear when the chicken is pierced with a knife. Remove from the oven and, when the pieces are cool enough to handle, strip off and discard the skin. Remove the meat from the bones. Discard the bones unless you wish to reserve them for stock (page 19). Proceed with the recipe. The chicken can be stored, covered, in the refrigerator for up to 24 hours.

## whole roast chicken

: 1 whole chicken
: Salt and freshly ground black pepper
: Softened butter

**preparation ::**

Preheat the oven to 400°F.

Rinse the chicken and pat it dry with paper towels. Season lightly with salt and pepper, inside and out, and rub the outside with softened butter. Place the chicken, breast side down, on a V-shaped rack in a roasting pan. After 15 minutes, turn it over on its back. Baste with the pan drippings several times. Roast the bird for a total of 50 minutes, or until a meat thermometer registers 180°F when inserted in the thigh, not touching the bone. Remove from the oven, and when the chicken is cool enough to handle, strip off and discard the skin. Remove the meat from the bones, and discard the bones or reserve them for stock (page 19). Refrigerate the chicken meat, covered, until ready to use. The chicken can be stored, covered, in the refrigerator for up to 24 hours.

15

# basicrecipes

## mayonnaise

Although you can use a good brand of purchased mayonnaise to make chicken salad, the rich flavor of homemade mayonnaise cannot be equaled. Making mayonnaise is a simple task that you can easily master. Once you have learned the technique, you may find it interesting to experiment with different oils and different types of vinegar or lemon juice.

If you are concerned that the eggs you use may not be salmonella free, I would suggest using a purchased mayonnaise, as I have found the recipes calling for partially cooking the egg not worth the trouble.

If there are strong flavors in your salad, you may want to choose a stronger oil. If your salad has more delicate flavors, a lighter oil, such as grapeseed, might be better. Many times a combination of oils works well, such as half olive oil and half vegetable oil, or you might want to add a little walnut oil.

Here is my preferred homemade mayonnaise.

**makes about 1¼ cups ::**

: 1 large egg, plus 1 large egg yolk

: 1½ teaspoons Dijon mustard

: 1 tablespoon fresh lemon juice
  or white wine vinegar

: Salt and freshly ground black pepper

: 1½ cups vegetable oil, or
  1 cup vegetable oil and
  ½ cup extra virgin olive oil

**to make mayonnaise in a food processor or a blender ::**

Place the whole egg, egg yolk, mustard, lemon juice or vinegar, salt, and pepper in the work bowl of the processor or blender. Process for 20 seconds to dissolve the salt and thicken the egg. With the motor running, start to add the oil very slowly, just a dribble at a time, increasing the flow as you see it beginning to thicken and become creamy. When all the oil has been added, taste and adjust the seasoning. If it has become too thick, add a drop or two of water and process to mix. Store the mayonnaise, covered, in the refrigerator.

**to make mayonnaise by hand ::**

Follow the machine method, using a bowl and a whisk. Anchor the bowl to the work surface by putting a damp towel underneath it.

If your mayonnaise curdles because the oil was added too quickly, all is not lost. Simply place an additional ½ teaspoon of mustard in a clean work bowl. Stir the curdled mixture and then, 1 tablespoon at a time, whisk it vigorously into the bowl with the mustard. Keep adding the curdled mayonnaise, 1 tablespoon at a time, mixing well after each addition. The end result should be a nice, creamy mayonnaise. Be sure to go slowly enough at first to allow the mayonnaise to emulsify, or thicken.

## vinaigrette

A basic vinaigrette dressing is the classic point of departure for many salad dressings. The general rule of thumb is 1 part vinegar or other acidic liquid such as citrus juice or wine to 3 parts oil. The mixture can be seasoned with herbs, spices, mustard, salt, and pepper. You may whisk the ingredients together in a bowl, or use a food processor or a blender. Adding mustard to the vinegar produces a smoother emulsion.

**makes about ⅔ cup ::**

: 3 tablespoons vinegar of your choice,
  such as red or white wine, tarragon, sherry,
  or balsamic vinegar, or 3 tablespoons fresh
  lemon juice

: ¼ teaspoon salt, or to taste

: Pinch of freshly ground black pepper

: 1 teaspoon Dijon mustard (optional)

: 2 teaspoons finely chopped rosemary,
  thyme, or oregano, or any herb of your
  choice (optional)

: ½ cup oil of your choice, such as olive,
  canola, or vegetable oil

In a small bowl, mix the vinegar, salt, pepper, and mustard, if using, with a whisk, or process them in a food processor or blender. (If you are using herbs, add them at this point.) Add the oil drop by drop, whisking or processing constantly, until an emulsion forms. The mixture will be cohesive. Refrigerate in a jar with a lid and shake well before using.

16

## toasted nuts

Many of the recipes in this book call for the addition of nuts, either in the salad itself or as a garnish. Although you may certainly use the nuts straight from the package, the process of toasting them adds considerably to their flavor and texture. Unless the recipe specifically calls for whole nuts, chop them before toasting. The cut sides of the nuts allow the oils to come to the surface, resulting in a richer flavor.

You may toast nuts in a skillet on top of the stove or on a baking sheet in the oven. You may also microwave them, but they need to be turned every 30 to 40 seconds, which I find tedious.

### to toast nuts in a skillet ::

This works best for a small quantity of ½ cup or less.

Warm a nonstick skillet over medium heat, add the nuts, and stir frequently until you see the first signs of browning. This should take 2 to 3 minutes. Take the nuts off the heat and immediately transfer them to a small bowl or plate, as they will continue to brown if left in the skillet. The skillet method works well with pine nuts and sesame seeds.

### to toast nuts in the oven ::

Preheat the oven to 350°F. Spread the nuts on a baking sheet and place them in the oven. Toast until they begin to brown and become aromatic, 6 to 8 minutes, checking them after 3 or 4 minutes and stirring them at that time. Remove from the oven and transfer the nuts to a bowl or plate.

Whether you toast them on the stove or in the oven, watch them very carefully, as their high fat content causes them to go from barely brown to burnt very rapidly.

## croutons

I enjoy my homemade croutons much more than the purchased variety. They are baked and then sautéed, producing a dry, crispy crouton. Once you taste the delightfully crunchy flavor of your own homemade croutons, you'll think twice before purchasing the box. You can adjust the flavor of the croutons to complement your salad by varying the herbs. These keep in a cookie tin for a week or frozen in a plastic container for a month.

### makes three cups ::

: 4 slices firm white toasting bread, such as Pepperidge Farm Toasting Bread

: 2 tablespoons unsalted butter (see note)

: ¼ teaspoon salt

: ¼ teaspoon freshly ground black pepper

: 2 tablespoons minced curly parsley

: 1 teaspoon dried herbs, such as thyme, tarragon, or oregano

Preheat the oven to 375°F. Trim the crusts from the bread and cut the slices into ½-inch cubes. On a baking sheet, spread the cubes in a single layer and bake until dry and golden, about 10 minutes. Remove from the oven. Melt the butter in a skillet over medium heat and add the croutons and the salt, pepper, parsley, and herb of your choice. Crumble the herb with your fingers as you add it to release the flavor. Sauté over medium heat, stirring, for 2 minutes. Remove from the burner and cool. Use the croutons immediately or store them in a cookie tin or sealed plastic container.

**note ::** *Unsalted butter will not burn as quickly as salted butter.*

17

## roasted peppers

Although you can buy jars of roasted red peppers at the supermarket, home-roasted peppers taste so much better that it's worth a little extra work. You also have the advantage of being able to roast yellow, orange, and green peppers that are not ordinarily available in jars. It's a simple process, and may be done a day or two ahead.

### to roast peppers in the oven ::

Preheat the broiler. Split the peppers in half and remove the ribs and seeds. Place the pepper halves, cut side down, on a baking sheet lined with aluminum foil and place them under the broiler. Broil the peppers until the entire surface is black and blistered, 8 to 10 minutes.

### to roast peppers over a gas flame ::

Leave the peppers whole. Spear a pepper on the end of a long fork. Char it over the open flame until it is blackened and blistered all over.

### to peel the peppers ::

Transfer the blackened peppers to a plastic or brown paper bag. Close the bag and let the peppers stand for about 10 minutes. Remove the peppers from the bag and peel away the charred skin. Use as directed in the recipe, or wrap the peppers in plastic and refrigerate for up to 3 days. You may place the peppers in a container, cover them with oil, and store them in the refrigerator for a week.

## chicken stock

There is no great mystique to making your own chicken stock, and the flavor rewards are many. Although purchased cans of chicken stock are readily available, many of them are too salty or have other additives such as flavor enhancers; just read the label. By having a few containers of good homemade chicken stock in your freezer, you'll have at the ready an instant base for many soups and sauces as well as a good poaching liquid for chicken.

If you poach chicken for the recipes in this book, strain and refrigerate or freeze the poaching liquid. You can use it again for poaching chicken. Each time you do so, the stock will become more enriched. You can also make a good stock from the leftover carcass of a roast chicken.

Here is a good chicken stock from scratch. Do not add the livers to the pot, as they will make the stock cloudy.

### makes eight to ten cups ::

: 3 pounds chicken wings, necks, and backs, or 1 chicken, 3 to 3½ pounds, cut up into 8 pieces

: 1 large onion, unpeeled, coarsely chopped

: 2 large carrots, unpeeled, coarsely chopped

: 2 stalks celery with leaves, coarsely chopped

: 5 sprigs curly parsley

: 1 large bay leaf

: ½ teaspoon dried thyme

: 1 teaspoon whole black peppercorns

: 15 cups cold water

Place the chicken parts in the bottom of a large kettle or stockpot.

Place the onion, carrots, celery, parsley, bay leaf, thyme, and peppercorns on top of the chicken. Add the water. Bring the mixture just to a boil, and reduce the heat. Skim off any scum that rises with a slotted spoon. Partially cover the pot to prevent too much evaporation, and let the mixture simmer for 2 to 3 hours, skimming the scum from time to time.

Strain the stock through a colander, pressing the juices from the vegetables with the back of a spoon.

Cool the stock to lukewarm, then refrigerate. After 8 hours, use a slotted spoon to remove any fat that has risen to the surface. Store the stock in the refrigerator for 3 days, or freeze it for up to 3 months.

19

chicken
salads
withmainly
chicken

The beautiful town of Belfast, Maine, sits on the rugged coast, at the head of Penobscot Bay. My grandfather, Lewis Greene, was at one time the mayor of Belfast, along with being the manager of Penobscot Poultry Company. Summer visits to my grandparents' house overlooking the bay were a real treat, highlighted by the annual Penobscot Poultry Festival. The festival offered, among other activities such as crowning the queen and the grand parade, a superb grilled chicken dinner. Served in large tents, the dinner consisted of half of a crispy grilled chicken cooked on huge grills known as "fire tables," a scoop of stuffing, a mound of crunchy cole slaw, and, of course, a dollop of cranberry sauce. The real queen of the festival was a variety of chicken known as the Cacklebird, which had more breast meat than any other chicken around. My grandfather proudly stated that when the Cacklebird trucks arrived at market in New York, very few other brands sold until there were no more Cacklebirds. There was always some chicken left after the big day, and my grandmother turned it into Cacklebird Salad.

# cacklebird salad

22

**serves six to eight ::**

: 2 whole chicken breasts (or 5 cups cubed cooked chicken)

: 1 cup chopped celery

: ¼ cup vinaigrette, homemade (page 16) or high-quality purchased

: Lettuce leaves for serving

: 4 medium tomatoes, quartered, for garnish

**dressing ::**

: 1 cup mayonnaise, homemade (page 16) or high-quality purchased

: 1 tablespoon Dijon-style mustard

: ½ teaspoon salt

: ½ teaspoon freshly ground black pepper

: 2 teaspoons celery seed

**preparation ::**

Poach the chicken according to the master recipe for poaching chicken (page 14). When it is cool enough to handle, remove any bones, skin, and visible fat and cut the chicken into ½-inch cubes. If you are using leftover chicken, cut it into ½-cubes, using just white meat or a combination of dark and white meat. Put the chicken and the celery in a large bowl and sprinkle it with the vinaigrette. Chill for 1 hour or more.

To make the dressing, in a separate bowl, mix the mayonnaise, mustard, salt, pepper, and celery seed.

Pour the dressing over the chicken and celery and toss gently but thoroughly. Refrigerate, covered, for up to 8 hours. When ready to serve, line a serving bowl or platter with lettuce leaves, turn the chicken salad out onto the leaves, and garnish with the tomato quarters.

**serves four to six ::**

: 1 whole chicken breast
(or about 2½ cups
cubed cooked white
meat; see note)

: 3 chicken thighs
(or about 1 cup cubed
cooked dark meat;
see note)

: 1 cup chopped celery

: 2 tablespoons
chopped red onion

: ½ cup dried cranberries

: ¼ cup chopped
flat-leaf parsley, plus
more for garnish

: ¼ cup chopped walnuts,
toasted (page 17)

: Red-leaf lettuce
leaves for serving

**dressing ::**

: ¾ cup mayonnaise,
homemade (page 16) or
high-quality purchased

: 2 tablespoons
maple syrup, preferably
Medium grade

: 2 teaspoons honey
Dijon mustard

: ¼ teaspoon curry
powder

Here in New Hampshire we use maple syrup in many ways. Maple syrup comes in several grades, and New England cooks prefer the Medium grade to the Fancy grade for cooking. After the flamboyant maple leaves have fallen and the deep of winter is upon us, any sign of spring is welcome. The first warm days of March, still accompanied by cold nights, signal the beginning of the maple syrup season. This salad celebrates the beginning of spring and the sugar houses' production of this unique New England product.

# new england maple chicken salad

**preparation ::**

If you are using the chicken breasts and thighs, roast them according to the master recipe for roasting chicken parts (page 15). When cool enough to handle, remove the meat from the bones, remove and discard the skin, and cut the chicken into 5-inch cubes.

Place the chicken in a large bowl, and add the celery, onion, dried cranberries, parsley, and walnuts. Set aside.

To make the dressing, place the mayonnaise in a small bowl and whisk in the maple syrup, mustard, and curry powder.

Pour the dressing over the chicken mixture, and toss gently but thoroughly. Cover and refrigerate for up to 24 hours. Place on a platter lined with red lettuce leaves, and garnish with chopped parsley. Serve chilled.

**note ::** *You may substitute the meat of 1 deli rotisserie chicken for the breast and thighs, if you prefer.*

23

# jo'sfriedchickensalad

My family has several wonder-women in its number. My sister Jo is not only a visiting nurse for the town of Hingham, Massachusetts; she is also a wife and mother of two active teenagers. Both Carlie and Greg agree that this salad is "awesome," when Mom has the time to make it. She volunteered this recipe as the family's pick for special occasions. Several of the steps may be done in advance, but the final frying and assembly should be done no more than an hour ahead.

**serves four to six (or two teenagers!) ::**

- 1 pound boneless, skinless chicken thighs or breasts, or ½ pound of each
- 1 cup plain yogurt
- 2 tablespoons ground cumin
- 2 teaspoons Worcestershire sauce
- 1 tablespoon hot pepper sauce
- 1½ pounds Yukon Gold potatoes
- ½ pound carrots
- ¼ pound green beans, haricots verts if available
- Salt

- 2½ cups panko crumbs (see note) or other fine dry breadcrumbs
- Vegetable or peanut oil for deep-frying
- ½ medium red onion, thinly sliced
- Greens of your choice for serving

**dressing ::**
- ¼ cup white wine vinegar
- Freshly ground black pepper
- 1 teaspoon hot pepper sauce
- 1 cup extra virgin olive oil
- ⅓ cup fresh cilantro leaves, minced

**preparation ::**

Cut the chicken pieces into ½-inch cubes and set aside. In a large bowl, mix the yogurt, cumin, Worcestershire sauce, and hot pepper sauce. Add the chicken pieces, and turn to coat. Cover the mixture with plastic wrap and refrigerate for at least 8 hours or overnight.

Peel the potatoes and cut them into ¼-inch julienne. Place them in a bowl of cold water so they won't discolor while you prepare the carrots.

*Continued*

24

*jo's fried chicken salad continued*

**preparation ::**

Cut the carrots into ¼-inch julienne and set aside. Snap the ends off of the beans, and cut them in half horizontally. Bring a pot of water to a boil, add salt, and boil the potato sticks until just tender, 4 to 6 minutes. Do not overcook. Lift them out of the water with a strainer, and run them under cold water to stop the cooking. In the same boiling water, cook the carrots for 2 to 4 minutes, lift them out with a strainer, and run under cold water. Cook the beans last, for about 2 minutes. Drain and run under cold water to set the color. Place all the vegetables in a large bowl. (The vegetables may be patted dry, placed in a bowl, and covered with plastic wrap until you are ready to proceed.)

Remove the chicken pieces from the marinade and pat dry with paper towels.

In a large plastic bag, combine the breadcrumbs and the dried chicken and shake well to coat the chicken. Remove the chicken pieces from the bag and place on a rack over a baking sheet. Refrigerate for 30 minutes to set the coating.

While the chicken is chilling, make the dressing. Whisk together the vinegar, pepper to taste, and hot pepper sauce. Whisk in the olive oil in a slow stream until an emulsion forms. Whisk in the cilantro. Set aside.

In a wok or a deep skillet, heat 1½ inches of the vegetable or peanut oil to 375° F. Use a deep-fat thermometer to check the temperature. Fry the chicken pieces in the hot oil until golden, about 1 minute or less. Transfer to paper towels to drain. Add the chicken and red onion to the vegetable mixture. Add the dressing and toss gently. Arrange the salad on a bed of greens and serve immediately.

**note ::** *Panko crumbs are Japanese-style breadcrumbs. They make an especially light and crunchy surface for fried foods such as the chicken in this recipe. They can be found in Asian specialty stores or in the Asian section of the supermarket.*

**serves two to four ::**

: 1 whole chicken breast
(or 2 to 2½ cups
cubed cooked chicken)

: 1 cooked lobster tail,
or 1 cup cooked
lobster meat (see notes)

: ½ cup finely
chopped celery

: ¼ cup sweet
pickle relish, drained

: Boston or Bibb
lettuce for serving

: 2 tomatoes, quartered,
for garnish (optional)

: 2 hard-boiled eggs,
quartered, for
garnish (optional)

**dressing ::**

: ½ cup mayonnaise,
homemade (page 16) or
high-quality purchased
(see notes)

: 1 tablespoon chopped
fresh tarragon,
or 1 teaspoon dried,
crumbled tarragon

: 1 teaspoon
fresh lemon juice

: Salt and freshly
ground black pepper

One Monday morning in summer, I found myself with a cooked lobster tail and some chicken, all left from the weekend's feasting. Like many New Englanders, I stretch my lobster as far as it will go. The result was a salad that combined the lobster and the chicken together, bound by a delicately flavored tarragon mayonnaise. I liked the salad so much that I now buy an extra lobster just to have the meat for this dish. You can serve the salad in the traditional way on a grilled hot dog roll if you prefer. The recipe can easily be expanded.

# poorman's lobsterroll salad

**preparation ::**

Poach the chicken according to the master recipe for poaching chicken (page 14). When cool enough to handle, remove any bones, skin, and visible fat. Cut the chicken into ½-inch cubes. Cut the lobster into cubes the same size. Place the chicken and lobster in a bowl. Add the celery and pickle relish, mix gently, and set aside.

To make the dressing, in a small bowl, whisk the mayonnaise together with the tarragon and lemon juice. Add salt and pepper to taste.

Pour the dressing over the chicken-and-lobster mixture and toss, gently but thoroughly. Cover and refrigerate for 1 hour or up to 8 hours. Line individual plates with Boston or Bibb lettuce leaves, and then mound the salad on the lettuce. Garnish with tomato sections and hard-boiled eggs, if desired.

**notes ::** *Lobster meat is available frozen; the thawed meat works well in this recipe. Use 1 cup of thawed frozen lobster meat, well drained and picked over for cartilage, in the salad.*

*If making your own mayonnaise, use tarragon-flavored vinegar for the acidic portion of the dressing. It will enhance the tarragon flavor of the dressing.*

27

The nine Common Man Family Restaurants run the length of New Hampshire, from Windham to Lincoln. Each one has its own individual style and menu, but the commonality is delicious, innovative food. The founder, Alex Ray, is known for his philanthropic efforts and gives back to the communities of New Hampshire by supporting many charities. In the summer, my friends and I often dine on the porch of one of the Common Man restaurants, the Boathouse Grille. As the sun dips into beautiful Meredith Bay and the town lights begin to twinkle, the day is complete with a plate of Chicken Caesar salad and a glass of buttery chardonnay. Executive chef Alan Barry has graciously provided this recipe so that you can enjoy it as well.

# theboathousegrillechickencaesarsalad

**serves eight ::**

: 2 heads romaine lettuce, torn into bite-sized pieces

: 1 cup croutons, home-made (page 17) or high-quality purchased

: 8 chicken breast halves, 5 to 6 ounces each, broiled or grilled, skin removed, boned, and sliced thinly on the diagonal

: 6 canned anchovies, drained, blotted dry, and minced (optional)

**dressing ::**

: 1 egg or ¼ cup pasteurized egg product (see note)

: ¼ cup fresh lemon juice

: 1 clove garlic, minced

: ½ teaspoon dry mustard

: 1 cup freshly grated Parmesan cheese

: 1 cup canola or vegetable oil

**preparation ::**

To make the dressing, in a bowl, mix together the egg, lemon juice, garlic, dry mustard, and Parmesan cheese. Slowly whisk in the oil until an emulsion forms.

Place the lettuce in a large bowl and toss with enough of the dressing to coat the leaves lightly. Toss in the croutons. Divide the salad among individual plates, and top with the grilled chicken slices and optional anchovies. Serve at once.

The greens may be cleaned and refrigerated in a plastic bag several hours ahead. The dressing may also be prepared several hours ahead and stored, covered, in the refrigerator. The chicken may be grilled, sliced, wrapped in plastic wrap, and refrigerated up to overnight.

**note ::** *Pasteurized egg product is found in the dairy section of the super-market. If you live in an area where the use of raw eggs is a concern, I recommend using this product.*

While visiting on Cape Cod with several "foodie" friends last summer, the conversation naturally turned to recipes. Dottie Sternberg, a lovely lady who is an avid mah-jongg player, shared this recipe that she serves at her mah-jongg get-togethers. It intrigued me and, upon trying it, I found it to be quick, easy, and quite delicious. She told me that Paul Newman's dressing was the key to the flavor. Paul Newman's contribution to mah-jongg parties is significant. Make sure the chicken breasts are the same size, or the cooked result will be uneven.

# dottie's mah-jongg chicken salad

**preparation ::**

Wash the chicken breasts and pat dry with paper towels. Season them on both sides with salt, pepper, and the garlic salt. Cook the breasts in a single layer in the microwave for 4 to 7 minutes per pound, depending on the microwave wattage. Turn them over halfway through. When they are done and cool enough to handle, remove the skin and any visible fat. Cut the breasts into ½-inch cubes, place in a shallow dish, and pour just enough of the dressing over the chicken to coat it, ½ to ¾ cup. Cover with plastic wrap and refrigerate the meat for 4 hours or up to overnight.

In a sieve, drain the cubes of any excess liquid and place them in a bowl. Add enough mayonnaise to coat the meat, then add the grapes and mix gently but thoroughly. Place the mixture in a serving bowl. Garnish with the walnuts and serve. (This salad can be refrigerated again for up to 8 hours before serving.)

**serves six ::**

: 4 boneless, skinless chicken breast halves

: Salt and freshly ground black pepper

: 1 teaspoon garlic salt

: 1 bottle (8 ounces) oil and vinegar dressing, such as Newman's Own Olive Oil and Vinegar

: ¼ cup mayonnaise or more, homemade (page 16) or high-quality purchased

: 1 cup red seedless grapes, cut in half

: ½ cup chopped walnuts, toasted (page 17)

**serves four ::**

: 3 chicken breast halves
  (or about 3½ cups
  cubed cooked chicken)

: 2 tablespoons
  vegetable oil

: Red-leaf lettuce leaves,
  for serving

: 2 tablespoons chopped
  cilantro for garnish

**dressing ::**

: 2 tablespoons chopped
  green onions, green
  and white parts

: 3 tablespoons drained
  canned diced water
  chestnuts (or fresh, if
  available)

: 1 tablespoon chopped
  unsalted peanuts

: ½ cup mayonnaise,
  homemade (page 16) or
  high-quality purchased

: 1 teaspoon lime juice

: ¼ teaspoon
  Asian sesame oil

: ¼ to ½ teaspoon
  prepared wasabi (see
  note)

: 1 teaspoon soy sauce

My daughter-in-law Lisa D. is another family wonder-woman. She has an excellent career, two perfectly adorable children, Jake and Sam, a wonderful husband, and she cooks!

Lisa and my son C.H. cook delicious and innovative meals every weekend, as relaxation from their demanding jobs. This salad is her recipe, handed to me on a Post-It Note when I told her I was working on this book. Its fresh flavors and ease of preparation make it a winner.

# lisad'sgrilledchickensalad

**preparation ::**

Preheat a gas grill, or start a charcoal fire. While the grill is heating, brush the breasts with the vegetable oil. Place the chicken breasts on the grill, and grill them over the hottest part of the fire. This should take no more than 3 to 4 minutes on each side, depending on the thickness of the breasts. When done, remove the chicken to a cutting board and allow it to cool while you prepare the dressing.

To make the dressing, in a small bowl, combine the green onions, water chestnuts, and peanuts. Mix in the mayonnaise, lime juice, sesame oil, wasabi to taste, and soy sauce.

When the chicken is cool enough to handle, remove any bones, skin, and visible fat. Cut the chicken into ½-inch cubes. Place it in a large mixing bowl, add the dressing, and mix gently but thoroughly. Cover and refrigerate for 2 hours or up to 8 hours. Line a platter with red-leaf lettuce leaves and mound the salad on the platter. Garnish with chopped cilantro before serving.

**note ::** *Prepared wasabi is a Japanese horseradish; it can be found in a tube at Asian groceries or in the Asian section of many supermarkets. It is strong, so know your guests' tolerance for heat.*

Years ago, Shillito's department store in Cincinnati, Ohio, offered an Italian week to promote the Italian goods that could be found in the store. The opening night was an Italian extravaganza, with music, entertainment, and refreshments on every floor. Since I was the cooking school director, it was my job to plan the food, all of which was to be taken from the book *Menus for Pasta* by the noted Italian cookbook author and teacher Anna Teresa Callen. Anna Teresa came and signed her book, and presided as an honored guest over a festive meal in the store's seventh-floor dining room. *Pollo al Verde*, a lovely preparation of chicken breasts in a vibrant green basil and parsley sauce, was served. To this day it is one of my favorites. The gracious Anna Teresa consented to the adaptation of her dish for this book. She suggests garnishing the platter with tomato slices or strips of roasted red and yellow pepper, if you desire.

# chicken salad verde annateresa

**serves six to eight ::**

:  3 whole chicken breasts (6 to 7 cups cubed cooked chicken)

:  Red-leaf lettuce leaves for serving

:  Tomato slices, or roasted red or yellow pepper strips (page 19) for garnish

**dressing ::**

:  1 cup loosely packed flat-leaf parsley

:  ½ cup loosely packed fresh basil leaves

:  1 clove garlic

:  1 tablespoon drained capers

:  2 to 3 cornichons, or 1 small sour pickle

:  1 stalk celery, coarsely chopped

:  ½ cup extra virgin olive oil

:  1 tablespoon red wine vinegar

:  Juice of ½ lemon (about 3 tablespoons)

**preparation ::**

Poach the chicken breasts according to the master recipe for poaching chicken (page 14). Reserve ¼ cup of the poaching liquid. When the breasts are cool enough to handle, remove any bones, skin, and visible fat. Cut the chicken into ½-inch cubes and place in a large bowl.

To make the dressing, in a food processor or blender, combine the parsley, basil, garlic, capers, cornichons, celery, oil, and vinegar. Purée until very smooth. If the sauce becomes too thick, add a little of the reserved poaching liquid. Taste the sauce and add lemon juice as needed.

Spoon the dressing over the chicken and toss gently but thoroughly. Arrange lettuce leaves on a platter and mound the salad in the middle. Garnish with tomato slices or roasted pepper strips. Serve immediately, or cover and refrigerate for up to 4 hours. Before serving, bring to room temperature.

# make-your-own
## chickensalad

Sam and Rosie's Café in my town of Center Harbor, New Hampshire, is a gathering spot for breakfast or lunch any time of the year. Located across the road from the town docks, it's a convenient spot for boaters to enjoy lunch on the porch. In the winter months, when the snow is deep and the lake frozen solid, the windows of the café steam up, and it's a cozy and inviting spot for a bowl of Rosie's excellent chowder. I asked Rosie about a recipe for chicken salad for this book, and she told me she didn't have one. "Just good mayonnaise and chicken, that's all. Some folks don't like celery, some don't like onion, so we just serve them the basic." After this conversation, I had an idea: Why not a "make-your-own" chicken salad? Just like a fondue party, this is a fun way to entertain a group of friends. Put out a large bowl of cubed chicken, dressed with an excellent mayonnaise, with the additions of your choice in smaller bowls. A platter of several types of lettuce leaves, some interesting breads, and it's a wonderful meal!

34

**serves six to eight
(can be increased) ::**

: 2 whole chicken breasts
  (or about 5 cups
  cubed cooked chicken)

: 1½ cups mayonnaise,
  homemade (page 16) or
  high-quality purchased

: Salt and pepper to taste

**suggested additions ::**

: Chopped green onion,
  green and white parts

: Grapes, red or green

: Chopped celery

: Chopped walnuts
  or almonds

: Chopped pickles

: Finely chopped herbs:
  parsley, tarragon, mint,
  or thyme

: Chopped, pitted
  olives, black or green

: Minced jalapeño
  pepper

: Chopped chutney

: Chopped green or
  red pepper

: Capers

: Selection of lettuce
  leaves

: Chopped apples, skin
  left on

: An assortment of
  spices, such as curry
  powder, cinnamon,
  red pepper flakes,
  cumin, ground ginger

: Chopped pears, skin
  left on

: Dried cranberries or
  raisins

: Orange sections,
  peeled

**preparation ::**

Poach the chicken according to the master recipe for poaching chicken (page 14). When it is cool enough to handle, remove any bones, skin, and visible fat. Cut the chicken into ½-inch cubes and place them in a large bowl. Add the mayonnaise and toss gently but thoroughly. Cover and refrigerate until serving time. When ready to serve, put as many of the optional additions as you wish in bowls or plates, surrounding the large bowl of chicken. Allow guests to mix and serve themselves. Don't forget the salt and pepper!

Caroline Russell is the owner of the Village Greenery, a florist shop in Meredith, New Hampshire. We were discussing my chicken salad project one day, and she volunteered her family's recipe for this classic mayonnaise chicken salad, which has been served at family get-togethers for generations. She told me nothing had been written down with specific amounts. "We just make it," she said. I've re-created the recipe from Caroline's description. I hope the family would approve.

# caroline'schickensalad

**serves six to eight ::**

: 1 chicken, 2½ to 3 pounds (or 4 to 5 cups cooked cubed chicken)

: ½ cup extra virgin olive oil

: 1 cup chopped celery

: 2 hard-boiled eggs, chopped (optional)

: 1 tablespoon drained capers, plus 2 teaspoons for garnish

: 1 cup (or more) mayonnaise, homemade (page 16) or high-quality purchased

: Juice of ½ lemon (about 3 tablespoons)

: Salt and freshly ground black pepper to taste

: Bibb or Boston lettuce leaves for serving

**preparation ::**

Poach the chicken according to the master recipe for poaching chicken (page 14). When it is cool enough to handle, remove the meat from the carcass and discard the skin. Cut the meat into ½-inch cubes, using both white and dark meat. Place the meat in a bowl and drizzle the olive oil over it, mixing it into the chicken. Cover and refrigerate overnight. The next day, remove the chicken from the refrigerator, and add the celery, chopped egg, if using, and 1 tablespoon of the capers. Fold in the mayonnaise and lemon juice gently but thoroughly. Add salt and pepper to taste. Refrigerate for up to 8 hours and serve chilled. When ready to serve, arrange the lettuce leaves of your choice on a platter and mound the salad in the middle. Garnish with the remaining 2 teaspoons of capers.

35

My friend Liz Lapham is an excellent cook. She comes by her talent naturally. Her mother, Ella McDowell, came to the United States from Scotland in 1922. She worked as a cook, settling in the posh town of Greenwich, Connecticut. Eventually she and her friend Sheila, another Scottish immigrant, formed a catering business, serving the wealthy families of the town. Liz remembers her mother using cheddar cheese in this recipe, but she has updated it with Brie, making it even more elegant.

# ella'schickensaladlog

**preparation ::**

Poach the chicken breast according to the master recipe for poaching chicken (page 14). When it is cool enough to handle, remove any bones, skin, and visible fat, and cut it into ¼-inch cubes.

Preheat the oven to 375°F. Lightly spray a baking sheet with nonstick cooking spray.

In a bowl, mix together the chicken cubes, Brie, bell pepper, green onions, mayonnaise, salt, and pepper.

Place the puff pastry on a lightly floured surface and roll out to approximately 10 inches by 12 inches.

Place the pastry on the sprayed baking sheet. Paint the entire surface of the pastry with the beaten egg, reserving about 1 teaspoon for the assembled log. Starting at the short (10-inch) end, spoon the filling in a 4-inch-wide strip down the center of the pastry.

Make cuts in the dough at 1-inch intervals, from the edge of the pastry sheet to the filling.

Bring the cut strips of dough across the filling, alternating from side to side, and seal by overlapping them. Brush the log lightly with the remaining beaten egg.

Bake for 20 minutes, until golden brown. Let rest for 10 minutes before serving. Cut with a serrated knife. Serve while still warm.

**serves three to four ::**

: 1 chicken breast half (or 1 to 1¼ cups cubed cooked chicken)

: 8 ounces Brie cheese, cut into ½-inch pieces

: ¼ cup diced red bell pepper

: ¼ cup chopped green onion, both green and white parts

: ⅓ cup mayonnaise, homemade (page 16) or high-quality purchased

: ½ teaspoon salt

: ¼ teaspoon freshly ground black pepper

: 1 sheet purchased puff pastry, thawed if frozen

: 1 egg, beaten

36

serves four to six ::

: 1 whole chicken, about 3 pounds (or about 4 cups cubed cooked chicken)

: 1½ cups thinly sliced celery

: 2 tablespoons diced red onion

: 1 tablespoon finely chopped parsley

: ½ cup slivered almonds, toasted (page 17)

: ½ teaspoon salt

: ¼ teaspoon freshly ground black pepper

: 2 tablespoons fresh lemon juice

: 1¼ cups mayonnaise, homemade (page 16) or high-quality purchased

: ½ cup grated sharp cheddar cheese

: ¾ cup crushed potato chips, preferably salt-and-vinegar flavor

·I do not know why this is always called a salad, but it is a 1950s classic and was part of every self-respecting cook's collection of chicken recipes. Although it was a ladies' luncheon favorite, now it might be served as an easy supper. It is an ideal dish to bring to a cooperative meal; not only does it reheat well, but it also tastes good at room temperature. I like to serve it with a platter of fresh citrus and avocado slices and some crusty bread. If you are making it ahead to transport, bring the crushed potato chips in a separate container and sprinkle them on just before putting the dish in the oven.

# chicken'n'chipshotsalad

**preparation ::**

Roast the chicken according to the master recipe for roasting chicken (page 15). When it is cool enough to handle, remove the bones, skin, and any visible fat, and cut it into ½-inch cubes.

Preheat the oven to 400°F. Butter or spray with nonstick cooking spray a 1½-quart shallow baking dish.

Combine the chicken, celery, onion, parsley, and almonds in a large bowl.

In a small bowl, combine the salt, pepper, lemon juice, and mayonnaise.

Combine the mayonnaise mixture with the chicken mixture, tossing gently but thoroughly. Turn the chicken into the prepared baking dish. Sprinkle the cheese over the top, and then do the same with the potato chips. Bake for 20 minutes, or until the top is slightly browned and bubbling. Serve immediately. (To reheat, place the dish in a 325°F oven for 15 minutes.)

38

You won't find the answer to the age-old conundrum here, but you will find the solution to what to do with your Easter eggs. The day after our annual Easter egg hunt I was confronted, upon opening the refrigerator, with a bowl of brightly colored eggs. You can use more or fewer eggs than called for, depending on what the bunny left you. For an elegant but quick and easy spring meal, just add some steamed asparagus, a good wheat bread, and a glass of white wine. I like adding pickle relish to the salad, but it is optional.

# whichcamefirst: thechickenortheegg? salad

serves four to six ::

: 3 chicken breast halves (or about 3½ cups cubed cooked chicken)

: 6 hard-boiled eggs

: ½ cup chopped celery

: ¼ cup chopped green onion, both white and green parts

: 2 tablespoons sweet pickle relish (optional)

: ¾ cup mayonnaise, homemade (page 16) or high-quality purchased

: 3 tablespoons chopped curly parsley for garnish

**preparation ::**

Poach the chicken according to the master recipe for poaching chicken (page 14). When it is cool enough to handle, remove any bones, skin, and visible fat, and cut the chicken into ½-inch cubes. Place it in a large bowl.

Shell the eggs and chop them coarsely. Add them to the chicken, along with the celery, green onion, and pickle relish if using. Add the mayonnaise, tossing gently but thoroughly. Cover and refrigerate for at least 1 hour or up to 8 hours. Just before serving, garnish with the chopped parsley.

39

While on a trip to China with my college alumnae group last year, we went to a wonderfully chaotic restaurant in Chongquing. We were all a little leery of the reptiles in cages waiting to be selected by more adventurous diners. You know what people say about rattlesnake meat—"it tastes just like chicken." But we were assured that our lunch was indeed chicken. I have reconstructed a close facsimile of that delicious dish.

# chinesegrilledchickensalad

**preparation ::**

To make the marinade, mix the soy sauce, fish sauce, sesame oil, five-spice powder, and the optional hot chile oil.

Place the chicken breasts, one at a time, in a gallon-size plastic bag and pound them with a cleaver or the bottom of a frying pan until they are no more than ¼ inch thick. Place them in a flat dish and pour the marinade over them. Marinate, refrigerated, for 30 minutes. Pre-heat a gas grill or start a charcoal fire. (You may also broil the chicken in the oven, turning the breasts after 4 minutes.) When the fire is ready, remove the chicken pieces from the marinade and grill them on the hottest part of the fire. This should take no more than 3 to 4 minutes on each side, depending on the thickness of the breasts. Remove the chicken from the fire, place it on a cutting board, and slice it diagonally into ½-inch-wide strips.

In a small bowl, mix together the olive oil and rice wine vinegar, pour over the shredded lettuce or cabbage, and toss gently. Place on a shallow platter.

Arrange the chicken strips over the shredded lettuce or cabbage. Sprinkle the toasted sesame seeds over all and tuck the green onion flowers in here and there. Serve immediately.

**note ::** *To make green onion flowers, the onions should be at least ½ inch thick at the root (the white part). Slice about 1½ inches off of the root end. With a small, sharp knife, cut from the center out to form a petal, and keep making these cuts all the way around the onion, keeping the cuts close together.*

*Place the onion flowers in a bowl of ice water for 5 minutes in the refrigerator, or until ready to serve.*

**serves six to eight ::**

:  6 boneless, skinless chicken breast halves, 4 to 5 ounces each

:  ¼ cup extra virgin olive oil

:  2 tablespoons rice wine vinegar

:  6 cups shredded iceberg lettuce or napa cabbage

:  2 tablespoons sesame seeds, toasted

:  6 green onion flowers (see note) for garnish

**marinade ::**

:  ½ cup soy sauce

:  1 tablespoon fish sauce

:  1 teaspoon Asian sesame oil

:  ¼ teaspoon Chinese five-spice powder

:  1 teaspoon hot chile oil (optional)

40

# chicken salads with vegetables and legumes

My daughter Lisa told me no collection of chicken salad recipes would be complete without her all-time favorite. I had completely forgotten the recipe, which, she reminded me, I served quite frequently during the steamy summers when we lived in Cincinnati, Ohio. Because of the town's proximity to the Ohio River, the weather can be very humid and uncomfortable. All the ingredients for this salad can be prepared in the cool of the morning and then tossed together just before serving.

# cincinnatisummerchickensalad

**serves six to eight ::**

: 2 whole chicken breasts (or about 5 cups cubed cooked)

: ¾ pound green beans, trimmed and cooked just until tender, drained and chilled

: 2 medium tomatoes, cut into 6 wedges each

: 3 cups chunked iceberg lettuce

: Lettuce leaves for serving

: 1 cup sliced radishes

: ¼ pound Swiss cheese, cut into ¼-inch-wide strips

: 4 slices bacon, cooked until crisp, drained, and crumbled

**dressing ::**

: 2 tablespoons fat from the cooked bacon

: 3 tablespoons ketchup

: Pinch of sugar

: ½ cup Vinaigrette (page 16)

**preparation ::**

Poach the chicken according to the master recipe for poaching chicken (page 14). When it is cool enough to handle, remove any bones, skin, and visible fat and cut the meat into ½-inch cubes. Set aside.

Place the beans in a large bowl.

To make the dressing, in a small bowl, whisk together the bacon fat, ketchup, sugar, and vinaigrette.

Add the cubed chicken to the beans, then add the tomatoes and chunked lettuce. If serving immediately, toss the dressing with the chicken, beans, and chunked lettuce. Line a serving platter with lettuce leaves, and mound the salad in the center. Top with the radish slices, cheese strips, and bacon.

If preparing the salad in advance, chill all of the ingredients, but do not toss them with the dressing until just before serving.

Lake Winnipesaukee stays frozen for a long time. So it is with great anti-cipation that we look forward every year to "Ice Out." It usually occurs in April and is declared official when it is determined that the *M/S Mount Washington* cruise boat can cruise the length of the lake, from Center Harbor to Alton Bay, without *Titanic* results. What better way to celebrate this rite of spring than with a festive salad bursting with south-of-the-border flavors?

# iceoutchickensalad

**serves eight ::**

: 2 whole chicken breasts (or about 5 cups cubed cooked chicken)

: 4 fresh tomatillos, husked and washed (see notes)

: ½ cup chopped celery

: ½ cup jicama, peeled and cut into small cubes (see notes)

: 1 jalapeño, seeds removed, finely chopped

: 1 ripe avocado for garnish

: 3 tablespoons lemon juice

: 1 cup corn chips, crumbled, for garnish

**dressing ::**

: 1 cup mayonnaise, homemade (page 16) or high-quality purchased

: ½ cup low-fat or regular sour cream

: ½ cup tomato-based salsa of your choice (see notes)

: Pinch of sugar

: ¼ cup chopped fresh cilantro

: Salt and freshly ground black pepper

**preparation ::**

Poach the chicken accord-ing to the master recipe for poaching chicken (page 14). When it is cool enough to handle, remove any bones, skin, and visible fat, and cut the chicken into ½-inch cubes. Transfer to a bowl and set aside.

Bring 2 cups of water to a boil in a small saucepan, add the tomatillos, and reduce the heat to a simmer. Cook gently for 5 to 6 minutes, or until they yield to gentle pressure. They will turn a dull green. Don't overcook them or they will burst. Remove the tomatillos from the water and, when they are cool enough to handle,

chop them coarsely. Add them to the chicken along with the celery, jicama, and jalapeño.

To make the dressing, in a bowl whisk together the mayonnaise, sour cream, and salsa. Add the sugar, cilantro, and salt and pepper to taste.

Pour the dressing over the salad and toss gently but thoroughly. Chill briefly, or refrigerate for up to 4 hours. Just before serving, peel and chop the avocado and sprinkle the lemon juice over it. Transfer the salad to a platter or bowl or a piece of Mexican pottery and garnish with the corn chips and avocado pieces. Serve at once.

**notes ::** *Tomatillos are not really tomatoes but are related to the Cape goose-berry. The husk encasing a tomatillo must be peeled off before using. If you are unable to find tomatillos, you may substitute a medium green tomato, but do not cook it.*

*Jicama, the tuber of a tropical vine used widely in Mexican cuisine, is now found in many American supermarkets. It is delicious raw or cooked. If you can-not find it, substitute an equal amount of additional celery.*

*There are many excellent salsas in the supermarket. Select one according to your heat tolerance.*

# chickenandcranberries withgreenpeamousse

If you are like me, finding a new holiday dish that is delicious and also easy is a godsend during the hectic Christmas season. By combining two favorite recipes, I came up with this elegant salad that is a hit at holiday parties.

**serves four to six ::**

**mousse ::**

: 1 cup boiling water

: 1 packet (¼ ounce) unflavored gelatin

: 2 cups cooked, drained peas, preferably small petits pois, fresh or frozen

: ½ teaspoon salt

: Pinch of freshly ground black pepper

: 1 cup sour cream

**salad ::**

: ½ cup dried cranberries

: 2 tablespoons brandy or hot water

: 1 pound smoked deli chicken (about 3 cups cubed)

: ¼ cup finely chopped celery

: 2 tablespoons chopped pecans, toasted (page 17)

: 3 green onions (both green and white parts), chopped, for garnish

: 2 tablespoons peas, thawed if frozen, for garnish

: ½ cup raw cranberries for garnish

**dressing ::**

: 1 tablespoon fresh lemon juice

: ¼ teaspoon salt

: Freshly ground black pepper

: ¾ cup mayonnaise, homemade (page 16) or high-quality purchased

**preparation ::**

To make the mousse, spray a 4-cup ring mold with nonstick cooking spray. Set aside. Pour the boiling water into a blender container or the work bowl of a food processor. Sprinkle the gelatin over the water. Cover and blend or process for 40 seconds. Uncover and add the peas, salt, and pepper. Blend or process for an additional 40 seconds. Uncover and add the sour cream. Blend or process just until the sour cream is incorporated.

Pour into the ring mold. Cover with plastic wrap and refrigerate until firm, about 3 hours or up to 24 hours.

To make the chicken salad, put the dried cranberries in a small bowl with the brandy or hot water and let them plump while you cut up the chicken. Cut the smoked chicken into ½-inch cubes. Place it in a bowl with the celery, pecans, and drained plumped cranberries.

To make the dressing, put the lemon juice, salt, and pepper to taste in a bowl, and whisk in the mayonnaise.

Pour the dressing over the chicken mixture and refrigerate for up to 24 hours.

To serve, unmold the mousse on a round platter (see note), and fill the center with the chicken salad, mounding it up attractively. Sprinkle with the chopped green onion and peas. Surround the mold with the raw cranberries. Serve at once.

**note ::** *I prefer to unmold my gelatin-based salads by filling the sink with hot water, dipping the mold in the water for 10 seconds, and then giving it a gentle shake. Invert the platter over the mold, and then turn the platter right side up. Before lifting the mold off, give it another gentle shake. It also helps to slightly moisten the platter before unmolding, so that you can center the mousse on the platter more easily.*

My children were always adventurous eaters, brought up on the rule of the "no thank you" helping. This rule came from my days as a Girl Scout camper, when one had to try everything but could request a small "no thank you" helping if the food offered didn't look appealing. Confirmed spinach haters will share Popeye's love of the vegetable when they taste this colorful salad. It has a wonderfully crunchy texture and is best prepared with the first tiny, tender spinach leaves of spring.

# popeyechickensalad

**serves six ::**

: 1 whole chicken breast (or about 2½ cups cubed cooked chicken)

: ¾ pound fresh spinach, or 1 bag (10 ounces) spinach leaves, or 2 bags (6 ounces each) baby spinach leaves, washed, dried, and torn if large

: 1 can (8 ounces) water chestnuts, rinsed, drained, and chopped

: 3 or 4 green onions, chopped (white and green parts)

: 1 cup fresh bean sprouts, rinsed and dried

: 4 slices bacon, cooked until crisp, drained, and crumbled

: 4 hard-boiled eggs, peeled and sliced

**dressing ::**

: ½ cup vegetable oil

: ⅓ (scant) cup sugar

: ¼ cup balsamic vinegar

: ¼ cup ketchup

**preparation ::**

Poach the chicken according to the master recipe for poaching chicken (page 14). When the chicken is cool enough to handle, remove any bones, skin, and visible fat. Cut it into ½-inch cubes. Place the chicken, spinach leaves, water chestnuts, green onion, bean sprouts, crumbled bacon, and slices of hard-boiled egg in a large bowl. If not serving immediately, store the salad, undressed but covered, in the refrigerator for up to 4 hours.

To make the dressing, in a small bowl blend the oil, sugar, vinegar, and ketchup together with a whisk.

Pour some of the dressing over the salad ingredients. (You may not need all of the dressing.) Toss the salad gently but thoroughly. Add more dressing if needed. The unused dressing may be stored in the refrigerator for up to 2 weeks.

Every Friday morning I walk with a group of seven other women "of a certain age," affectionately named WWW (Wonderful Women Walking) by a member's husband.

I can't remember when we started, but we have remained fast friends over the years, and we share each other's life experiences. New grandchildren and birthdays are celebrated, current events are discussed, and discussions of ailments are allowed ten minutes, no more. We set out from the Inn at Mills Falls, where Lake Waukewan tumbles into Lake Winnipesaukee. Rain, snow, heat, we stride through it all. After forty-five minutes of vigorous walking, we adjourn to the Waterfall Café for coffee and bagels. Occasionally we dine together. I had the group for lunch one day, and since we try to maintain healthy diets, I concocted this salad of lentils and chicken. Lentils, rich in protein, are a wonderful background for the chicken and fruit. It "walked" away with honors from the WWW.

# thewww'schickenandlentilsalad

**serves six to eight ::**

: 1 whole chicken breast (or 2 to 2½ cups cubed cooked chicken)

: ¾ cup dried lentils (see note)

: 1 large tart apple, such as Granny Smith

: Juice of ½ lemon (about 3 tablespoons)

: ¼ cup minced red onion

: ½ cup chopped walnuts, toasted (page 17)

: Red-leaf lettuce leaves for serving

**dressing ::**

: Juice of ½ lemon (about 3 tablespoons)

: ¼ teaspoon ground turmeric

: ½ teaspoon curry powder

: ¼ teaspoon ground cinnamon

: Salt and freshly ground black pepper

: ⅔ cup grapeseed oil

**preparation ::**

Poach the chicken breast according to the master recipe for poaching chicken (page 14). When it is cool enough to handle, remove any bones, skin, and visible fat and cut the meat into ½-inch cubes. Set aside.

Place the lentils in a medium-sized saucepan and add 2 cups cold water.

Bring to a boil, lower the heat, and simmer, uncovered, for about 30 minutes. Most of the water will be absorbed. Taste for doneness. When done, drain and set aside.

To make the dressing, place the lemon juice in a small bowl. Whisk in the turmeric, curry powder, and cinnamon. Add salt and pepper to taste, and whisk until all the seasonings have dissolved. Slowly add the oil, whisking as you pour, until an emulsion forms.

Core the apples, but do not peel them. Chop them coarsely and then toss them with the lemon juice.

In a large bowl, combine the chicken, warm lentils, apple, onion, and walnuts. Pour the dressing over the mixture and toss gently but thoroughly. Cover with plastic wrap and refrigerate for up to 2 hours, or serve immediately. This salad is most attractive served on red-leaf lettuce.

**note ::** *Lentils need no soaking. According to Russ Parsons in* How to Read a French Fry, *they should always be started in cold water so the starch will swell more gradually and thoroughly. There are generally three types of lentils available. The ordinary brown lentils used in this recipe take about 30 minutes to cook. Red lentils, used in Indian dishes, cook in about 10 minutes. The French Le Puy lentils, which are a gray-green color, take the longest to cook— about 40 minutes.*

50

**serves six to eight ::**

:  6 chicken thighs
   (or about 3 cups cubed
   cooked chicken)

:  2 cans chickpeas
   (19 ounces each),
   rinsed and drained
   (about 4 cups)

:  2 medium tomatoes,
   peeled, seeded, and
   chopped

:  2 cloves garlic, finely
   minced

:  3 tablespoons finely
   chopped red onion

:  3 tablespoons chopped
   flat-leaf parsley

:  ½ cup crumbled feta
   cheese

:  2 tablespoons pine
   nuts, toasted
   (page 17), for garnish

**dressing ::**

:  3 tablespoons red
   wine vinegar

:  Salt and freshly
   ground black pepper

:  ½ cup extra virgin
   olive oil

According to John Ayota in *The Glutton's Glossary*, there is no etymological connection between chickpeas and chickens. In some parts of the world, chickpeas are known as *ceci* or garbanzo beans. Chickpea flour is used in Mediterranean dishes such as *socca*, or chickpea flour pancakes. It is a staple in Indian and Middle Eastern cuisine. Hummus is also made from puréed chickpeas. They have been around for thousands of years, a testament not only to their nutritive value but also to their wonderful flavor. Chickpeas are available both dried and canned. The dried peas require a long soak, but the canned variety is quite acceptable and works well in this salad. This is a wonderful salad for potluck meals, as it holds up well. I call for flavorful dark meat in this recipe, but you may certainly use other parts of the chicken or leftover roast chicken.

# chickpea and chicken salad

**preparation ::**

Poach the chicken thighs according to the master recipe for poaching chicken (page 14). When they are cool enough to handle, remove any bones, skin, and visible fat. Cut the meat into ½-inch cubes. Place the chicken in a large bowl. Add the chickpeas, tomatoes, garlic, onion, parsley, and cheese.

To make the dressing, in a small bowl, whisk together the vinegar and salt and pepper to taste.

Slowly whisk in the olive oil until an emulsion forms. Pour the dressing over the chicken-and-bean mixture, and toss gently but thoroughly. Serve at once, or cover and refrigerate for up to 24 hours. Just before serving, garnish with the pine nuts. Serve chilled or at room temperature.

51

My daughter Lisa is a graduate student at Harvard University. When she is not working on her dissertation, she is cooking for her family. She finds great enjoyment and diversion in working in the kitchen. At a farmer's market in Cambridge last summer, she was quite taken with the beautiful green and yellow beans. So taken, she told me, that she bought way too many. The result was this summer salad, cool and refreshing, served with a tangy tarragon dressing.

# lisal'schickenandtwo-beansalad

**preparation ::**

Poach the chicken breasts according to the master recipe for poaching chicken (page 14).

While the chicken is poaching, bring a saucepan of water to a boil and add the beans. Cook just until crisp-tender, 4 to 5 minutes. Drain and refresh under cold water to stop the cooking and set their color.

When the chicken is cool enough to handle, remove any bones, skin, and visible fat and cut the meat into ½-inch cubes. Put the chicken in a bowl with the celery, onion, radishes, and beans.

To make the dressing, in a small bowl, whisk the lemon juice with salt and pepper to taste. Whisk in the sour cream and mayonnaise and finally the tarragon and parsley.

Pour the dressing over the chicken mixture and toss gently but thoroughly. Cover and refrigerate for up to 1 hour. Arrange on a platter or in a bowl and serve chilled. The components can be made early in the day and assembled just before serving.

**serves four to six ::**

: 3 chicken breast halves (or about 3½ cups cubed cooked chicken)
: ½ pound fresh green beans, ends removed, cut in half horizontally
: ½ pound fresh wax (yellow) beans, ends removed, cut in half horizontally
: ¼ cup chopped celery
: 2 tablespoons chopped red onion
: ½ cup sliced radishes

**dressing ::**

: 1 tablespoon fresh lemon juice
: Salt and freshly ground black pepper
: ½ cup regular or low-fat sour cream
: ½ cup mayonnaise, homemade (page 16) or high-quality purchased
: 2 tablespoons chopped fresh tarragon, or 2 teaspoons dried, crumbled tarragon
: 2 tablespoons chopped curly parsley

52

# creativekitchencobbsalad

When the Lazarus Department Store in Cincinnati opened the Creative Kitchen Cooking School, I was appointed director. The first event was an open house for the media, where luncheon would be served. I opted to serve Cobb salad, not only because it is delicious, but also because it looks impressive, feeds a lot of people, and has an interesting story. Robert Cobb originally created the salad in 1936 for his famous restaurant in Hollywood, the Brown Derby. It seems he created it from leftovers—in a sense, it was a chef's salad.

A forerunner of today's popular chopped salad, it has stood the test of time. The cooking school went on to win the Best in Cincinnati award for its 45-minute noontime Lunch 'n' Learn class, due partly, I'm sure, to the media's pleasure with the opening dish. I have updated the dressing with the buttery flavor of grapeseed oil.

### serves eight ::

: 1 whole chicken breast (or about 2½ cups finely diced cooked chicken)

: 2 ripe avocados

: 1 tablespoon fresh lemon juice

: ½ head iceberg lettuce, chopped

: ½ head red-leaf or chicory lettuce, chopped

: ½ head romaine lettuce, chopped

: 8 ounces sliced bacon, cooked until crisp, drained, and crumbled

: 3 hard-boiled eggs, chopped

: ½ cup (4 ounces) Roquefort or good-quality blue cheese, crumbled

: 2 medium ripe tomatoes, peeled, seeded, and diced

: ½ cup chopped green onion, both white and green parts

### dressing ::

: ⅓ cup white wine vinegar

: 1 tablespoon fresh lemon juice

: 1 teaspoon salt

: 1 teaspoon freshly ground black pepper

: ½ teaspoon sugar

: 2 teaspoons Worcestershire sauce

: ½ teaspoon dry mustard

: 1 tablespoon minced shallot

: 1 cup grapeseed oil

### preparation ::

Poach the chicken breast according to the master recipe for poaching chicken (page 14). When it is cool enough to handle, remove any bones, skin, and visible fat and cut the chicken into fine dice. Set aside.

To make the dressing, in a bowl, whisk together the vinegar, lemon juice, salt, pepper, sugar, Worcestershire sauce, and dry mustard. When the salt is dissolved, whisk in the shallot and grapeseed oil.

Cut the avocados in half, and remove the peel and the pits. Dice the avocados, place them in a small bowl, and sprinkle with the lemon juice. Combine the greens and toss them with ½ cup of the dressing.

To assemble the salad, choose a large salad bowl or platter. Arrange the greens on the bottom of the bowl. Arrange the diced chicken in a strip across the lettuce. Then arrange a row each of the crumbled bacon, eggs, cheese, tomatoes, and avocados. Sprinkle with the chopped green onion. Drizzle a little more dressing over the salad, and present it at the table. Toss the salad gently but thoroughly, and serve on individual plates at once. You may prepare each of the ingredients of the salad, except the avocados, as much as 24 hours ahead and store them, covered, in the refrigerator.

Recently, I had a lobster BLT sandwich at a local restaurant. It was a wonderful combination of flavors and textures. I began to think about what other ingredients could be combined to give the old standby a new twist. Since I was already working on this book, of course chicken came to mind. Here is the result, easily made in any quantity. You can find smoked chicken or turkey at the deli counter of your supermarket. Served with a frosty glass of iced tea, the wrap is a perfect quick lunch for a busy weekend. Iceberg is the traditional choice of lettuce for a BLT, but feel free to use any other lettuce, chopped, for this wrap (see photo, page 6).

**for each wrap ::**

: 1 wheat or white flour tortilla (10 inches in diameter)

: ¼ cup plus 1 tablespoon mayonnaise, home-made (page 16) or high-quality purchased

: ½ cup (4 ounces) diced smoked chicken or turkey

: ½ medium ripe tomato, seeds removed and diced

: 1 cup shredded iceberg lettuce (or lettuce of choice)

: 4 slices high-quality bacon, cooked, drained, and crumbled

# bacon, lettuce, and tomato chicken salad wrap

**preparation ::**

Place the tortilla on a work surface, and spread it with 1 tablespoon of the mayonnaise.

In a bowl, combine the chicken, tomato, lettuce, and bacon with the remaining ¼ cup mayonnaise. Spread the salad mixture on the tortilla. Pick up one side of the tortilla and roll it up, jelly-roll fashion. Cut it at an angle into two sections. Serve immediately, or wrap in plastic wrap and refrigerate for up to 2 hours.

55

One hot Sunday in August, I stopped at Moulton's farm stand on my way home from church and was delighted to see the first of the knobby fingerling potatoes and the slender, bright green haricots verts. My menu plan for Sunday dinner changed immediately. Instead of the intended roast chicken, green beans, and potatoes, with a platter of fresh tomato slices as a salad, I concocted a salade niçoise, using the same ingredients but much more suited to the weather. The various components of this composed salad can be made in the cool of the morning and then assembled and dressed just prior to serving time. I like to arrange it in a large, shallow bowl. When you want to pull out all the stops with a showy summer dish, this is it!

# chickensaladniçoise

**serves six to eight ::**

: 3 chicken breast halves (or about 3½ cups diced cooked chicken)

: 1 pound fingerling potatoes (or an all-purpose potato such as Yukon Gold)

: Salt

: 2 tablespoons red wine vinegar

: 1 pound haricots verts (or the slenderest green beans you can find)

: Boston or romaine lettuce leaves, for serving

: 4 ripe medium tomatoes, quartered

: 3 or 4 hard-boiled eggs, shelled and quartered

: 6 to 8 flat anchovy fillets, drained and blotted dry (optional)

: ½ cup black olives, preferably niçoise, pits removed

: 2 tablespoons drained capers

**dressing ::**

: Salt and freshly ground black pepper

: 3 tablespoons red wine vinegar or fresh lemon juice

: 2 tablespoons chopped shallot

: 1 clove garlic, minced

: 1½ teaspoons Dijon mustard

: ¾ cup extra virgin olive oil

**preparation ::**

Poach the chicken according to the master recipe for poaching chicken (page 14). When the meat is cool enough to handle, remove any bones, skin, and visible fat. Cut the chicken into ¼-inch dice. Refrigerate while preparing the remainder of the salad.

Rinse the fingerling potatoes but do not peel. Place them in a saucepan large enough to accommodate them, and cover with cold water by 2 inches. Add a good pinch of salt, and bring the potatoes to a gentle boil. Boil, uncovered, for about 10 minutes. Pierce them with a knife to test for doneness. Drain them in a colander and set aside. When the potatoes are cool enough to handle, cut them into ¼-inch slices, dropping the slices into a bowl. Sprinkle them with 2 tablespoons vinegar.

*Continued*

57

*chicken salad niçoise continued*

**preparation ::**

Wash the beans, and remove their tops and tails. Place 4 cups of water in a saucepan, bring to a boil, and add the beans. If you are using haricots verts, cook for no more than 3 minutes. If your beans are larger, boil until one is tender to the bite but not soggy, 5 to 6 minutes. Drain in a colander and immediately refresh under very cold running water.

To make the dressing, in a small bowl, combine some salt and pepper. Add the vinegar or lemon juice and whisk until the salt dissolves. Add the shallot, garlic, and mustard and then slowly add the oil, whisking well as you pour, until an emulsion forms. Taste and correct for seasoning.

In a bowl, toss the diced chicken with ¼ cup of the dressing, but do not saturate it.

Gently toss the potatoes with about ¼ cup of the dressing, or just enough to moisten them. They should be glistening but not drenched. Sprinkle 2 or 3 tablespoons of dressing over the beans if serving right away. Otherwise, reserve the dressing until serving time, as the beans will discolor if dressed too early.

When ready to serve, arrange the lettuce leaves on a platter. Sprinkle a little dressing on them. Arrange the potato mixture in the center, and then place the dressed beans in bundles, like spokes in a wheel, with the potatoes as the center. Place mounds of the dressed chicken between the bean bundles. Tuck the tomato wedges in next to the chicken, and add the egg sections at intervals. Sprinkle a little dressing over the tomatoes and eggs. Arrange the optional anchovies in the same pattern as the beans. Sprinkle the olives and capers over all. Serve at once. A crusty baguette is nice with this salad.

Ever since we went to Greece with the children, many years ago, I have been smitten by Greek food. We chartered a boat and sailed in and out amongst the islands in late August. The cloudless azure sky, the sparkling water, and the gentle breezes were so enchanting that even the usual brother-and sister-sniping ceased. We would anchor in coves known only to our guide Dimitri. We would swim and then we would eat, and oh how we would eat! The juiciest of ripe tomatoes, tangy feta cheese, plump black olives, fish and chicken grilled on the portable grill. Ever since then, when we have a really hot spell, I cook Greek. When the children still lived at home, they would say, "It must be hot; there goes Mom, into her Greek phase again!" The flavors of this salad evoke sunny memories.

# greekchickensalad

**serves four to six ::**

- 2 whole chicken breasts
- ½ cup olive oil
- Juice of ½ lemon (about 3 tablespoons)
- 1 teaspoon dried oregano (see note)
- ½ teaspoon salt
- ½ teaspoon freshly ground black pepper
- 3 cloves garlic, coarsely chopped
- 2 large, ripe tomatoes, peeled, seeded, and chopped
- ½ English cucumber, chopped
- ½ medium red onion, thinly sliced
- ¾ cup crumbled feta cheese
- ¾ cup kalamata or other black olives, pitted and coarsely chopped
- Fresh oregano sprigs for garnish (optional)

**dressing ::**

- 2 tablespoons fresh lemon juice
- 1 teaspoon dried oregano
- Salt and freshly ground black pepper
- ⅓ cup extra virgin olive oil

**preparation ::**

Place the chicken breasts in a shallow pan or dish. Mix together the olive oil, lemon juice, oregano, salt, pepper, and garlic. Pour the mixture over the chicken and let the breasts marinate for 30 minutes. Prepare a charcoal fire or a gas grill, or turn on the broiler. Remove the breasts from the marinade and pat dry. Place them on the grill or under the broiler. Grill the chicken, turning once after about 4 minutes, until it is just cooked through, about 9 minutes in all. Remove the chicken from the grill and when it is cool enough to handle, remove any bones, skin, and visible fat and cut the meat into ½-inch cubes. Place the chicken in a large bowl.

To the chicken, add the tomatoes, cucumber, onion, cheese, and olives.

To make the dressing, in a small bowl, whisk together the lemon juice, oregano, and salt and pepper to taste. Slowly add the oil, whisking as you pour, until an emulsion forms.

Pour the dressing over the chicken mixture and toss gently but thoroughly.

Place the salad in a large bowl and garnish with oregano sprigs, if desired.

Cover and refrigerate for up to 4 hours, or serve at once.

**note ::** *Oregano is one herb that, when used in a marinade or salad dressing, is more flavorful dry than fresh. Be sure to "disturb the herb" for maximum flavor by crushing it in the palm of your hand before using. This releases the full flavor.*

59

**serves six to eight ::**

: 2 whole chicken breasts (or about 5 cups shredded cooked chicken)

: 2 red bell peppers, roasted and peeled (page 19), or 2 bottled roasted red peppers

: 1¼ pounds sugar snap peas, strings removed, or 2 packages (10 ounces each) frozen sugar snap peas, cooked according to the package directions

: 2 tablespoons sesame seeds, toasted (page 17)

**dressing ::**

: 3 tablespoons red wine vinegar

: ¾ teaspoon salt

: ½ teaspoon freshly ground black pepper

: 1 tablespoon Dijon mustard

: ½ cup extra virgin olive oil

About the second or third week of June, Moulton Farm, in Meredith, New Hampshire, hangs out the sign "Peas Are Here." The shell peas, which require shelling, are delicious, but for this salad I like to use the tender sugar snaps, which are eaten whole, pod and all. I cannot get enough of these tiny green morsels, and I confess that as I drive away from the farm stand my hand dips in and out of the bag of peas, as I bite into the succulent pods. This colorful salad may be assembled several hours ahead but should not be dressed until you are ready to serve, to keep the peas from discoloring.

**preparation ::**

moulton farm
sugarsnapchickensalad

Roast the chicken according to the master recipe for roasting chicken parts (page 15). When it is cool enough to handle, remove any bones, skin, and visible fat, cut the whole breasts in half, and then cut each half in thirds. Using your fingers, pull apart the pieces into shreds. (This is easier to do if the chicken is still slightly warm.) Place the shredded chicken in a large bowl and set aside.

Cut the peppers into strips about ¼ inch wide. Add the peppers to the chicken.

If you are using fresh peas, take a paring knife and string the peas by starting at the top or stem end of the pea and running the knife down the seam of the pea, pulling the string off.

Place 3 cups of water in a 2-quart saucepan. Have a bowl of cold water standing by. Bring the water to a boil, and drop in the peas. Cook for 1 minute after the water returns to the boil. Drain and plunge the peas at once into cold water to retain their color.

When the peas have cooled, add them to the bowl with the pepper strips and chicken. If not serving immediately, store the salad, undressed but covered, in the refrigerator for up to 4 hours.

To make the dressing, in a small bowl, combine the vinegar, salt, pepper, and mustard, and whisk to dissolve the salt. Gradually whisk in the oil to form an emulsion.

When ready to serve the salad, toss the dressing with the pea, pepper, and chicken mixture, gently but thoroughly.

Turn the salad into a serving bowl or onto a platter, and sprinkle the sesame seeds over it. Serve immediately.

In the 1960s, you would have been hard pressed to open a church or Junior League cookbook and not find some version of the ubiquitous layered salad, clearly a forerunner of today's popular chopped salad. In revisiting this classic, I've made a few changes to bring it up to date. Its obvious advantage is that the preparation must be done ahead. Perhaps a whole new generation of cooks will rediscover what was enjoyed in the past. You can create your own signature dish by varying the types of lettuce, vegetables, and cheese used; however, the lettuce should be a sturdy variety.

# seven-layerchickensalad

**preparation ::**

Poach the chicken according to the master recipe for poaching chicken (page 14). When cool enough to handle, remove any bones, skin, and visible fat and shred the chicken meat. Set aside.

To make the dressing, in a small bowl, mix together the mayonnaise and sugar.

In a large, clear glass salad bowl, toss the shredded iceberg and chopped romaine lettuces together. On top of the lettuce, layer the shredded chicken, then spread ½ cup of the dressing over the chicken. Layer the celery, red bell pepper, green bell pepper, water chestnut, onion, and finally the peas. Spread the remaining dressing over the vegetables to cover. Sprinkle with the grated cheese. Cover the bowl tightly with plastic wrap and chill for at least 8 hours or overnight. Just before serving, remove the wrap and top with the bacon crumbles, egg, and tomato. Do not toss. Serve with salad servers long enough to reach the bottom of the bowl.

**dressing ::**

: 1½ cups mayonnaise, homemade (page 16) or high-quality purchased

: 1 tablespoon sugar

**serves six to eight ::**

: 1 whole chicken breast (or 2 to 2½ cups shredded cooked chicken)

: ½ small head iceberg lettuce, shredded

: ½ head romaine lettuce, inner leaves coarsely chopped

: 1 cup finely chopped celery

: 1 medium red bell pepper, seeded, deribbed, and chopped

: 1 medium green bell pepper, seeded, deribbed, and chopped

: 8 canned water chestnuts, drained and sliced

: ½ cup finely chopped red onion

: 1 package (10 ounces) frozen petits pois (small peas), thawed and drained (but not cooked)

: 1 cup (4 ounces) grated Romano cheese

: 8 ounces lean bacon, cooked, drained, and crumbled

: 1 hard-boiled egg, cut into wedges

: 1 medium tomato, cut into wedges

# the best chicken salad no one remembers eating

**serves six to eight ::**

: 3 whole chicken breasts

: 3 cups chicken stock, homemade (page 19) or high-quality purchased

: 1 cup canned crushed tomatoes

: 2 dried mild chiles, preferably ancho or New Mexico, stemmed and seeded

: ½ medium onion, chopped

: 2 cloves garlic, sliced

: 1 bay leaf

: 3 tablespoons extra virgin olive oil

: 1 tablespoon cider vinegar

: 1 can (15 ounces) chickpeas, rinsed and drained

: 1½ cups Monterey jack cheese, diced

: ½ cup chopped roasted mild green chile, preferably New Mexico or Anaheim, fresh, frozen, or canned

: ½ yellow, orange, or red bell pepper, diced

: 2 small tomatoes, preferably Roma or Italian plum, diced

: 2 Hass avocados, cubed

: ¼ cup minced fresh cilantro

: Lettuce leaves for serving

This particular salad is a favorite of my daughter Lisa. She tells me that it comes from *The Border Cookbook* by Cheryl Alters Jamison and Bill Jamison, under the title Chicken Salpiçon. She first made it for her husband Bill, when he was due home from the hospital to recover from knee surgery. She made it again one Mother's Day for me. I had just returned from China and was suffering from acute jet lag. Apparently Bill and I each enjoyed it, but since neither of us was in a state to remember it, she calls it "the best chicken salad that no one remembers." We tried it again when feeling better, and yes, it is delicious. It is an excellent do-ahead dish.

**preparation ::**

In a Dutch oven or large saucepan, combine the chicken, stock, tomatoes, dried chiles, onion, garlic, and bay leaf. Bring the mixture to a boil; reduce the heat to a low simmer, and cover. Poach the chicken in the liquid for 20 to 25 minutes, until cooked through. Remove the chicken with a slotted spoon and set it aside until cool enough to handle. Discard the bay leaf.

Transfer the cooking liquid to a blender in batches and purée. Return the liquid to the pan and simmer over medium heat for 35 to 45 minutes, until reduced to about 1½ cups. Add the oil and vinegar to the reduced sauce to make a dressing.

Remove any bones, skin, and visible fat from the chicken and shred or cube it. Place it in a glass dish. Pour about two-thirds of the dressing over the chicken and refrigerate for least 2 hours, or overnight. Drain the chicken of any remaining dressing. Mix the chicken with the chickpeas.

Arrange the chicken mixture on a decorative platter. Scatter the cheese, chopped chile, bell pepper, diced tomatoes, avocados, and cilantro over the salad attractively and drizzle some of the remaining dressing on the top. Tuck lettuce leaves around the platter and serve.

63

chicken
saladswith
fruit

A student in one of my classes in Cincinnati gave this recipe to me years ago, and I've been making it ever since. The pleasing combination of curry and chicken are found in many salad recipes, but the tangy taste of fresh pineapple lifts this salad out of the ordinary. It is particularly pretty when served in hollowed-out pineapple shells. Fresh pineapple is a must; the taste of canned pineapple is too sweet and the texture not as pleasing. Diced white meat of roast turkey works very well here also.

# curriedchutneychickensalad

**serves six to eight ::**

: 2 whole chicken breasts (or about 5 cups cubed cooked chicken)

: 1 cup seedless white grapes, cut in half

: ½ fresh pineapple, peeled, cored, and cut into cubes

: Greens of your choice for serving

: ½ cup chopped pecans, toasted (page 17)

: ½ cup thinly sliced green onions, white and green parts

**dressing ::**

: ⅓ cup bottled Major Grey's chutney, large pieces chopped

: 1 teaspoon curry powder

: 1 cup mayonnaise, homemade (page 16) or high-quality purchased

: 1 tablespoon grated lime zest

: ¼ cup fresh lime juice

: ½ teaspoon salt

**preparation ::**

Roast the chicken according to the master recipe for roasting chicken parts (page 15). When it is cool enough to handle, remove the skin from the chicken. Pull the meat off the bones and cut it into ½-inch cubes. Place the meat in a large bowl. Add the grapes and pineapple.

To make the dressing, in a bowl, whisk together the chutney, curry powder, mayonnaise, lime zest, lime juice, and salt.

Pour the dressing over the chicken mixture. Toss gently but thoroughly. At this point, you may refrigerate the salad for up to 3 hours, or turn it out onto a platter lined with lettuce leaves, chill briefly, and serve. (If made more than 3 hours in advance, the dressing becomes runny.) Sprinkle the pecans and green onions over the salad before serving.

# chickensaladpourpre

"Véronique" in classic French cuisine indicates the presence of green grapes in a wine sauce. This salad originally called for green grapes and was called Salade Véronique until I forgot to buy green grapes and purchased the red variety instead. My ever-practical assistant, Liz, said, "Call it chicken salad *pourpre* instead." That remark sent me into gales of laughter as I remembered my student days in Paris and the French elocution lessons I took, where I had to repeat *"La lune, toute ronde et couleur de pourpre"* but could not pronounce "purple" in French for the life of me. I always started giggling, which made my fellow students join in and provoked a sharp rebuke from Mademoiselle, the teacher. With purple or green grapes, this salad is a winner for a crowd.

**preparation ::**

Poach the chicken according to the master recipe for poaching chicken (page 14). When cool enough to handle, remove any bones, skin, and visible fat, and cut the chicken into ½-inch cubes. Place the chicken in a large bowl and add the water chestnuts, celery, pineapple, and grapes.

To make the dressing, place 2 cups of the mayonnaise in a medium bowl.

Whisk in the lemon juice, curry powder, and salt and pepper to taste.

Pour the dressing over the chicken mixture, and toss gently but thoroughly. Add another ½ cup mayonnaise if desired. Cover and refrigerate for up to 4 hours. This salad may be served individually in a Bibb lettuce cup, garnished with some of the toasted almonds, or on a large platter lined with lettuce leaves, garnished with the almonds.

**serves twelve to fifteen ::**

- 3 whole chicken breasts (or 6 to 7 cups cubed cooked chicken)
- 1 can (8 ounces) water chestnuts, drained and sliced
- 2 cups chopped celery
- 1 fresh pineapple, peeled, cored, eyes removed, and cut into 1-inch chunks
- 2 pounds seedless red grapes, washed and cut in half
- Bibb lettuce leaves for serving
- 2 cups slivered almonds, toasted (page 17), for garnish

**dressing ::**

- 2 to 2½ cups mayonnaise, homemade (page 16) or high-quality purchased
- 2 tablespoons fresh lemon juice
- 1 tablespoon curry powder
- Salt and freshly ground white pepper

**preparation ::**

Poach the chicken according to the master recipe for poaching chicken (page 14). When it is cool enough to handle, remove any bones, skin, and visible fat. Cut into ½-inch cubes.

In a large bowl, combine the chicken, apple, pear, grapes, celery, raisins, and 3 tablespoons of the walnuts. Refrigerate while you make the dressing.

To make the dressing, in a small bowl, mix together the mayonnaise, sour cream, honey, and lime juice.

Pour the dressing over the chicken mixture and toss gently but thoroughly.

Turn the salad out on a bed of lettuce leaves, garnish with the remaining 2 tablespoons nuts and the cheese, if using, and serve, or refrigerate up for to 1 hour.

Something about the name "Waldorf" conjures up elegance, sophistication, and the glamour of New York. I remember going to the Waldorf-Astoria hotel as a young girl and being completely in awe of the famous Peacock Alley, which at that time was a promenade in the hotel where the rich and famous could be spotted sporting the latest couture. Waldorf salad became a signature dish of the grand old hotel during the latter part of the nineteenth century. Here is an updated, low-calorie version with chicken that would make a lovely early fall luncheon or supper.

# waldorfchickensalad

**serves six ::**

: 2 whole chicken breasts (or about 5 cups cubed cooked chicken)

: 1 medium Red Delicious apple, unpeeled, diced

: 1 medium Anjou or Bosc pear, unpeeled, diced

: 1 cup seedless red grapes, halved

: ¾ cup diced celery

: ⅓ cup golden raisins

: 5 tablespoons chopped walnuts, toasted (page 17)

: Lettuce leaves for serving

: ½ cup crumbled blue cheese for garnish (optional)

**dressing ::**

: ½ cup low-calorie mayonnaise

: 1½ cup low-fat sour cream

: 1½ teaspoons honey

: 1½ teaspoons fresh lime juice

I like to prepare this salad in the dead of winter, when everyone needs a pick-me-up. The luscious fruits in this dish are now available year round in the supermarkets. You may vary the fruits by adding kiwi, papaya, or grapefruit, according to what is available in your store. You probably won't use all of the dressing on the salad. Save it for another day and use it over fresh spinach leaves. Served with warm cornbread, this salad is the sure cure for the winter blues.

# citruspoppyseedchickensalad

serves six to eight ::

: 1 pound deli smoked chicken, thickly sliced, cut into ½-inch cubes

: 1 firm-ripe mango, peeled, pitted, and cut into ½-inch cubes

: 1 navel orange, peeled, pith removed, and sectioned

: 1 Moro or blood orange, peeled, pith removed, and sectioned

: 1 avocado, peeled, pitted, and cut into ½-inch cubes

: 1 tablespoon fresh lemon juice

: Lettuce leaves for serving

: 1 star fruit (carambola), cut horizontally into ¼-inch slices for garnish (optional)

: ½ cup slivered almonds, toasted (page 17), for garnish

dressing ::

: ½ cup sugar

: 1 teaspoon dry mustard

: ½ teaspoon salt

: 2 tablespoons grated onion

: ⅓ cup cider vinegar

: 1 cup vegetable oil

: 1 tablespoon poppy seed

**preparation ::**

Place the chicken and mango cubes in a large bowl. Cut the orange sections in half and add to the chicken mixture. Sprinkle the avocado cubes with lemon juice and add them to the bowl.

To make the dressing, in a medium-sized bowl, mix together the sugar, dry mustard, and salt. Stir in the grated onion and 2 tablespoons of the vinegar, whisking until smooth. Gradually beat in the oil and the remaining vinegar. Add the poppy seed. Whisk until the dressing is smooth. You may also make this in a jar. Cover the jar and shake well before using.

Pour ½ cup of the dressing over the chicken mixture, and toss gently but thoroughly. Add more dressing if the salad seems dry. Line a serving platter with the lettuce leaves. Mound the salad on the platter and garnish with slices of star fruit, if desired, and the toasted almonds.

Another attractive presentation is to serve the salad in hollowed-out avocado shells, as in the Avocado Chicken Salad (page 74). Garnish as described above.

# bird of paradise chicken salad

One cold and snowy day I ventured down to the local supermarket and there, in the floral area, was a canister holding several elegant bird of paradise flowers, fresh from a clime far more tropical than mine. Their tall, stately heads of brilliant orange plumage took my mind off the sleet and snow outside. As I walked through the produce section, I fantasized what it would be like to be where those flowers had come from, right at that very moment. Short of that, perhaps something tropical for dinner? Today, even in frozen New England, we have access to tropical fruits year round. While they don't approach the juicy, lush flavor they have in their native climate, they make a pleasant break from the long days of winter. Here is a tropical chicken salad that can be made most anywhere.

**serves six to eight ::**

- 1 whole chicken breast (or about 2½ cups cubed cooked chicken)
- 1½ cups peeled, cored, and cubed fresh pineapple (½-inch cubes)
- 1 cup red seedless grapes, halved
- 2 ripe mangos, peeled and cubed
- 1 ripe papaya
- Lettuce leaves for serving
- 6 or more clusters of red grapes for garnish

**dressing ::**

- ¾ cup mayonnaise, homemade (page 16) or high-quality purchased
- ¼ cup fresh orange juice
- 2 tablespoons grated orange zest
- ½ cup chopped macadamia nuts, toasted (page 17)

**preparation ::**

Poach the chicken breast according to the master recipe for poaching chicken (page 14). When it is cool enough to handle, remove any bones, skin, and visible fat, and cut the meat into ½-inch cubes. Place the chicken in a large bowl along with the pineapple cubes, grape halves, and mango cubes. If you are not serving the salad immediately, cover and refrigerate the chicken mixture for up to 2 hours. If you refrigerate the mixture longer, the pineapple tends to give off its juices.

To make the dressing, in a small bowl, whisk together the mayonnaise, orange juice, and zest. Stir in ¼ cup of the nuts.

Pour the dressing over the chicken-and-fruit mixture, and toss gently but thoroughly.

Peel the papaya, using a vegetable peeler. Cut it in half, remove the seeds, and then cut it vertically into even slices. Line a serving platter with lettuce leaves, and mound the chicken mixture in the middle of the platter. Arrange the slices of papaya around the chicken, alternating with grape clusters. Sprinkle the remaining nuts over the salad. Serve immediately.

73

On the spur of the moment one Fourth of July, I invited friends to come and watch the fireworks display from my porch overlooking Lake Winnipesaukee. All I had on hand were three ripe avocados and some chicken breasts. I hollowed out the avocado shells, filled them with a chicken salad enrobed in a creamy dressing, and garnished the salads with slices of avocado. It was an ideal dish for that special occasion.

# avocadochickensalad

**preparation ::**

Poach the chicken breasts according to the master recipe for poaching chicken (page 14). When they are cool enough to handle, remove any bones, skin, and visible fat, and cut them up into ¼-inch cubes. Place the chicken in a large bowl and add the celery. Set the chicken mixture aside.

To make the dressing, in a small bowl, whisk together the mayonnaise, shallot, lemon juice, garlic salt, hot pepper sauce, parsley, and capers. Add salt and pepper to taste.

Pour enough of the dressing over the chicken mixture to moisten it. You may not need all of the dressing. Cut the avocados in half and remove the pit. Lift the flesh from the shell by sliding a spoon between the skin and the flesh, reserving the shells. Chop 2 of the avocados into small cubes and sprinkle with some of the lemon juice from the halved lemon. Add the chopped avocado to the chicken mixture, tossing gently but thoroughly. Slice the remaining avocado into 6 long slices and sprinkle with lemon juice.

Pile the chicken mixture into the shells and garnish each with an avocado slice and the chopped egg. Serve at once.

You may prepare the chicken mixture several hours ahead and refrigerate it, covered, until ready to serve, but do not cut up the avocados any more than 30 minutes before serving, as they will darken.

**note ::** *Hass avocados have a pebbly skin and are dark green in color. Avocados are picked unripe and ripen after picking. When you select a ripe avocado at the market, it should yield slightly to gentle pressure.*

**serves six ::**

: 3 chicken breast halves (or about 3½ cups of cubed cooked chicken)

: ½ cup finely chopped celery

: 3 ripe avocados, preferably Hass (see note)

: 1 lemon, cut in half

: 2 hard-boiled eggs, finely chopped, for garnish

**dressing ::**

: 1 cup mayonnaise, homemade (page 16) or high-quality purchased

: 1 shallot, finely chopped

: 1 tablespoon fresh lemon juice

: 1 teaspoon garlic salt

: 1 teaspoon hot pepper sauce

: 2 tablespoons finely chopped curly parsley

: 1 tablespoon drained chopped capers

: Salt and freshly ground black pepper

chapter 5 ::

# chicken
## salads with
## pasta, rice,
## and grains

Summer brings glorious music to the mountains of New Hampshire in the form of the New Hampshire Music Festival. Musicians from around the world come to our area of the state for a six-week series of concerts. In my capacity as hospitality chair for the council of Friends of the Festival, I served this salad to a group engaged in a fund-raising project. The salad, from *The Hay Day Cookbook*, is an all-time favorite of mine because it can be made a day ahead. Many thanks to Alex Van Rensselaer and everyone at Hay Day Market for letting me include this recipe here.

# hayday'sspicychickensalad

**serves eight to ten ::**

: 2 whole boneless chicken breasts (or about 5 cups sliced cooked chicken)

: 1 bunch green onions, chopped, with part of the green tops

: 12 ounces vermicelli, or other very thin pasta, cooked and drained

: ⅓ cup sesame seed, plus 2 tablespoons for garnish, toasted (page 17)

: ¼ pound snow peas, fresh or frozen, trimmed and blanched

: ¼ cup water chestnuts, sliced (optional)

: ¼ cup unsalted cashews (optional)

: Romaine lettuce leaves for serving

**dressing ::**

: ¼ teaspoon minced garlic

: 3 tablespoons tahini (ground sesame seed paste; see notes)

: 3 tablespoons Asian sesame oil

: ¼ cup soy sauce

: 1 tablespoon red wine vinegar

: 1 tablespoon tamari (see notes)

: 1 tablespoon hot chile oil (see notes)

: ¾ cup safflower oil

**preparation ::**

Poach the chicken breasts according to the master recipe for poaching chicken (page 14). When cool enough to handle, remove any bones, skin, and visible fat and cut the breasts into ⅜-inch strips. Place the strips in a large bowl. Add the green onions, vermicelli, and ⅓ cup of the sesame seed. Toss gently.

To make the dressing, in a medium bowl, whisk together the garlic, tahini, sesame oil, soy sauce, vinegar, tamari, and hot chile oil. Slowly add the safflower oil, whisking well as you pour.

Pour the dressing over the chicken mixture and toss gently but thoroughly. (This is easily done with your hands.) Refrigerate the salad for up to 24 hours. Just before serving, gently mix in the snow peas and the optional water chestnuts and cashews. Place the romaine on a large shallow platter, and turn the salad out onto the lettuce. Garnish with the remaining 2 tablespoons toasted sesame seed.

**notes ::** *Tahini can be found in the import section of most supermarkets.*

*Tamari is a thicker, more intense Japanese version of soy sauce. Both tamari and hot chile oil can be found in the Asian section of the supermarket.*

My family has called this salad "the church lady" salad ever since I presented it several years ago at my church in Hingham, Massachusetts. My mother was an ardent Altar Guild member, and had volunteered my services to give a cooking demonstration as a program for the churchwomen. After my talk, we adjourned to the undercroft for a luncheon prepared from my recipe by the lunch committee. As the guest speaker, I was served first, and all eyes were on me as I took the first bite. My teeth chomped down on a very hard, pointy object, but I smiled gamely as I raised my napkin to my lips and discreetly removed the pop-up timer! Only my mother was the wiser, as I slipped the napkin to her under the table. The salad, minus the timer, can be increased to feed a large group. It is necessary to make the salad at least eight hours ahead to allow the flavors to blend.

# churchladychickensalad

## serves six ::

: 3 chicken breast halves (or about 3½ cups cubed cooked chicken)

: 2 cups warm cooked rice, preferably long-grain

: ¼ cup minced green onion

: 1 scant teaspoon curry powder

: 1 teaspoon Beau Monde seasoning (see note)

: 2 tablespoons vegetable oil

: 2 tablespoons white wine vinegar

: 1 cup diced green bell pepper

: ¾ cup mayonnaise, homemade (page 16) or high-quality purchased

: ¼ to ½ cup slivered almonds, toasted (page 17)

: Red-leaf lettuce leaves or hollowed-out tomatoes for serving

## preparation ::

Poach the chicken according to the master recipe for poaching chicken (page 14). When cool enough to handle, remove any bones, skin, and visible fat, and cut the chicken into ¼-inch cubes. Cover and store in the refrigerator until needed.

Place the warm rice in a large bowl.

In a small bowl, mix together the green onion, curry powder, and Beau Monde seasoning. Add to the rice and blend well.

In the same bowl, blend the vegetable oil and white wine vinegar. Pour over the rice mixture and let stand overnight.

The next day, add the bell pepper and the mayonnaise to the rice mixture, then add the chicken and almonds and blend gently but thoroughly. Chill for up to 6 hours before serving.

Serve on a bed of red-leaf lettuce leaves or in hollowed-out tomatoes.

**note ::** *Beau Monde seasoning is a blend of spices called for in many older recipes. It is made by Spice Islands.*

serves six to eight ::

: 1 cup quinoa

: 2 cups chicken stock,
  homemade (page 19) or
  high-quality purchased

: 1 whole chicken breast
  (or about 2½ cups
  cubed cooked chicken)

: ½ cup golden raisins

: ½ cup julienned
  dried apricots

: ¼ cup pine nuts,
  toasted (page 17)

: 2 teaspoons
  minced fresh ginger

: Romaine lettuce
  leaves or other greens
  for serving

dressing ::

: 3 tablespoons white
  wine vinegar

: ½ teaspoon salt

: Freshly ground black
  pepper

: ½ to 1 teaspoon
  curry powder (adjust
  to your taste)

: ⅓ cup canola oil

The healthful properties of quinoa (pronounced *keen-WA*) have been known for more than 3,000 years. A basic food of the Incas, it is still a principal food crop in many areas of South America. Relatively unknown in this country until recently, it can now be found in the rice/legume section of the supermarket. It is high in protein, a good source of calcium, and, when mixed with other ingredients, tastes good. Be sure to rinse the quinoa in a sieve under cold running water if you are not sure whether it has been prewashed, as it will have a bitter taste if left unwashed.

# chickenquinoasalad

**preparation ::**

Rinse the quinoa well under cold running water and drain. In a medium saucepan, bring the chicken stock to a boil, add the quinoa, lower the heat, and cook, covered, until tender, 12 to 15 minutes. Most, if not all, of the liquid should be absorbed. Drain off any remaining liquid and let the quinoa cool.

Poach the chicken according to the master recipe for poaching chicken (page 14). When cool enough to handle, remove any bones, skin, and visible fat, and cut it into ¼-inch cubes.

In a medium bowl, mix the chicken, quinoa, raisins, apricots, pine nuts, and ginger.

To make the dressing, place the vinegar in a small bowl. Whisk in the salt until dissolved. Add pepper and curry powder to taste. Whisk in the canola oil.

Pour the dressing over the chicken mixture, and toss gently but thoroughly. Cover and refrigerate for up to 8 hours. Serve chilled on a platter of romaine leaves or other attractive greens.

81

Couscous, originally from North Africa, has become popular here, not only with vegetarians but also with people seeking an alternative to pasta, rice, and potatoes. It is actually very much like pasta. According to *Webster's New World Dictionary of Culinary Arts*, couscous is "small, spherical bits of semolina flour that are rolled, dampened and coated with a finer wheat flour." The French discovered it while in North Africa and brought it back to Europe. It is traditionally cooked in a couscousière, a sort of double boiler with perforations, to accompany a stew of meat or vegetables, which is cooked in the bottom part of the pot. Fortunately for us, there is a good couscous on the market that can be made in an ordinary saucepan in as little as five minutes. It is equally delicious warm or chilled.

# couscouschickensalad

**serves six to eight ::**

: 6 chicken thighs (or about 3 cups cubed cooked chicken)

: ⅔ cup chopped red onion

: ¼ cup finely chopped cilantro

: 1 medium tomato, peeled, seeded, and chopped

: ⅓ cup chopped green bell pepper

: ½ cup chopped curly parsley

: ½ cup chopped celery

: 4 cloves garlic, minced

: 1 box (10 ounces) plain couscous

: 2 cups chicken stock, either homemade (page 19) or high-quality purchased

: Romaine lettuce leaves for serving

: ¼ cup pine nuts, toasted (page 17), for garnish

**dressing ::**

: 3 tablespoons red wine vinegar

: ½ teaspoon ground cumin

: ½ teaspoon curry powder

: ¼ teaspoon salt

: Freshly ground black pepper

: ½ cup grapeseed oil

**preparation ::**

Poach the chicken according to the master recipe for poaching chicken (page 14). When cool enough to handle, remove any bones, skin, and visible fat, and cut the chicken into ¼-inch cubes. Place the chicken in a large bowl and add the onion, cilantro, tomato, bell pepper, parsley, celery, and garlic. Toss gently and set aside.

*Continued*

83

**preparation ::**

Prepare the couscous according to the directions on the box, using the chicken stock as the cooking liquid. When the couscous is cooked and slightly cooled, add it to the chicken mixture.

To make the dressing, in a small bowl, combine the vinegar with the cumin, curry powder, salt, and pepper to taste, stirring to allow the salt to dissolve. Whisk in the grapeseed oil.

Pour the dressing over the chicken mixture and toss gently but thoroughly. Cover and refrigerate for up to 8 hours. Line a bowl or a platter with romaine leaves, and mound the salad on the leaves. Serve chilled or at room temperature, garnished with pine nuts.

While this is not a chicken salad in the truest sense of the word, it makes use of the delicious chicken sausages available in the supermarket. They are sold in several different flavors. I have used the version made with sun-dried tomato in this recipe. You may substitute any of the other varieties, using the same proportions. There are many intriguing shapes of pasta available as well. I like to use a small shell shape in this salad, as the dressing becomes trapped in the curl of the shell. Be sure to cook the pasta just until done al dente; it should not be mushy.

# chickensausageandpastasalad

**serves six to eight ::**

: 2 cups (6 ounces) pasta, preferably shell shaped

: 1 tablespoon extra virgin olive oil

: 1 package (12 ounces) chicken sausage (sun-dried tomato or other flavor), broiled, grilled, or pan-fried, cut into ½-inch slices and each slice quartered

: ¼ cup chopped red bell pepper

: ¼ cup chopped green bell pepper

: ¼ cup chopped red onion

: ½ cup freshly grated Parmesan cheese

: Salt and freshly ground black pepper

: Whole basil leaves for garnish (optional)

**dressing ::**

: 3 tablespoons red wine vinegar

: ¼ teaspoon salt

: ¼ teaspoon freshly ground black pepper

: ½ cup extra virgin olive oil

: ¼ cup chopped fresh basil

**preparation ::**

Cook the pasta according to the package directions. Drain and sprinkle with the olive oil.

In a large bowl, place the cooked sausage pieces, cooked pasta, bell peppers, onion, and cheese. Toss gently to mix.

To make the dressing, in a small bowl, combine the vinegar, salt, and pepper. Whisk until the salt is dissolved. Slowly pour in the olive oil, whisking as you pour, until an emulsion forms. Stir in the chopped basil.

Pour the dressing over the sausage-and-pasta mixture, and toss gently. Add salt and pepper to taste. Cover and refrigerate for up to 24 hours. Serve chilled, garnished with basil leaves, if you wish.

85

# camelbackpulled
# chickensalad

The delightful Royal Palms Hotel in Scottsdale, Arizona built in the Spanish colonial style, was once the private residence of a wealthy family from upstate New York. It is now host to those who come to enjoy Arizona's sunny climate. One day in January, I had lunch on the terrace under a leafy canopy. The view of the neat rows of orange trees and the sparkling fountains was surpassed only by an excellent warm chicken salad. I have re-created the dish, but I leave it to you to create the atmosphere.

**serves four ::**

: 1 whole chicken, about 3 pounds (or 1 deli rotisserie chicken of the same size)

: 8 ounces farfalle pasta or other shape of your choice

: 1 tablespoon extra virgin olive oil

: 6 cups mesclun salad mix

: ¼ cup drained julienned sun-dried tomatoes packed in oil

: 4 thin slices fontina cheese, about 4 inches by 4 inches

**dressing ::**

: 2 tablespoons balsamic vinegar

: Salt and freshly ground black pepper

: ⅓ cup extra virgin olive oil

**preparation ::**

Roast the chicken according to the master recipe for whole roast chicken (page 15). When cool enough to handle, remove the skin and shred or "pull" both the white and dark meat off the chicken carcass. If using a deli rotisserie chicken, remove the skin and shred the meat. Set aside.

Bring 8 cups of water to a boil, add the farfalle, and cook until done, 10 to 11 minutes. Drain, and toss with the olive oil. Set aside.

Preheat the oven to 500°F.

To make the dressing, place the balsamic vinegar in a small bowl. Add salt and pepper to taste, whisking until dissolved. Slowly add the oil, whisking as you pour, until an emulsion forms.

In a medium-sized bowl, toss the mesclun with the dressing. Divide among 4 individual plates. Top the greens with the farfalle, then sprinkle the sun-dried tomato strips over the farfalle.

Allowing about 1 cup of shredded or "pulled" chicken per serving, place the chicken in neat individual bundles on a baking sheet sprayed lightly with nonstick cooking spray. Place a slice of cheese on top of each of the chicken bundles. Slide the baking sheet into the hot oven and cook just until the cheese begins to melt (about 2 minutes). Remove the sheet from the oven. Using a spatula, place a chicken cheese bundle on each plate of pasta and greens. Serve immediately.

You may assemble the chicken cheese bundles up to 4 hours ahead and refrigerate, covered. Remove from the refrigerator 30 minutes before cooking. Do not melt the cheese until just before serving. The pasta may also be cooked ahead.

Chicken has always had a great affinity for rice, especially in the South. My good friend Maxiene Glenday has the good fortune to spend a lot of time during the winter months in Florida, where she came across this recipe. It makes an elegant, yet not too caloric, salad. She serves it to New Hampshire friends in the summer months on individual plates lined with beautiful red lettuce from the local farm stand. It is always well received.

# maxiene'swildriceandchickensalad

**serves six ::**

- : 3 chicken breast halves (or 3½ cups finely diced cooked chicken)
- : ½ cup sliced green onion, white and green parts
- : 1 cup chopped pecans, toasted (page 17)
- : 1 cup long-grain and wild rice packaged blend, cooked according to package directions and cooled
- : Red-leaf lettuce leaves for serving

**dressing ::**

- : ⅔ cup plain yogurt
- : 1½ tablespoons fresh lemon juice
- : 3 tablespoons extra virgin olive oil
- : Salt and freshly ground black pepper

**preparation ::**

Poach the chicken according to the master recipe for poaching chicken (page 14). When the chicken is cool enough to handle, remove any bones, skin, and visible fat.

Cut the chicken into ¼-inch cubes. Place it in a large bowl, and add the green onion, pecans, and rice blend. Set aside.

To make the dressing, in a small bowl, whisk together the yogurt, lemon juice, and olive oil. Add salt and pepper to taste.

Pour the dressing over the chicken mixture, and toss gently but thoroughly. Cover and refrigerate for 1 hour or up to 8 hours. Serve on individual plates lined with red-leaf lettuce leaves.

**serves six to eight ::**

: 1 deli rotisserie chicken (or about 4 cups shredded roast chicken)

: 1 pint grape tomatoes, halved

: 1 box (10 ounces) frozen green peas, thawed but uncooked

: 2 stalks celery, chopped

: ¼ cup chopped green onion, both green and white parts

: 3 cups (6 ounces) dried pasta, preferably the wheel shape

: 1 tablespoon extra virgin olive oil

: ½ cup freshly grated Parmesan cheese

**dressing ::**

: ¼ cup red wine vinegar

: 1 teaspoon Dijon mustard

: 1 clove garlic, minced

: ½ teaspoon salt

: Freshly ground black pepper

: ½ cup extra virgin olive oil

Every June there is a phenomenon in the Lakes Region of New Hampshire called Motorcycle Week. More than 50,000 bikers from all over the country arrive on their Harleys, Hondas, and Kawasakis. They come from all walks of life: doctors, lawyers, firemen, and veterans. When I ran Watch Hill Bed and Breakfast, I had a group of wonderful people who returned year after year. At the end of the day, we sometimes gathered on the front porch and discussed, amongst other things, food. Here is their favorite chicken salad recipe, no doubt because of the pasta wheels.

# motorcycleweekchickensalad

**preparation ::**

If using the deli chicken, remove the skin and pull the meat from the bones. Shred the meat. Place the shredded chicken meat in a bowl. To the chicken add the tomatoes, peas, celery, and green onion. If not serving immediately, add the peas just before serving.

Cook the pasta according to the package directions. Drain and toss with the oil. Add the Parmesan cheese and toss again. When the pasta is cooled to room temperature, add it to the chicken mixture.

To make the dressing, in a small bowl, whisk together the vinegar, mustard, minced garlic, salt, and pepper to taste. Add the olive oil, whisking until it is incorporated. Pour the dressing over all, and toss gently but thoroughly. Cover and refrigerate for up to 8 hours. Serve chilled.

89

On the first Saturday of August, our church in Meredith, New Hampshire, has its annual fair. Everyone pitches in. There are homemade crafts as well as attic treasures for sale. Homemade jams, jellies, herb vinegars, breads, and baked beans grace the food tables. Following the fair, the workers' reward is the annual church picnic. We gather by the lake, and everyone brings a contribution. The picnic tables are laden with bowls of salad, casseroles, juicy watermelon, cakes, and many kinds of cookies. Joe LaFrance grills hot dogs and burgers and tops them with his tasty blend of sautéed peppers and onions. I like to bring this salad because I can make it early on fair day. It holds up well and is delicious.

# tortellinichickensalad

**serves eight to ten ::**

: 3 chicken breast halves

: 4 tablespoons extra virgin olive oil, divided

: 2 cloves garlic, minced

: 2 packages (9 ounces each) cheese tortellini, cooked according to the package directions

: 1 red bell pepper, roasted (page 19) and chopped

: 3 stalks celery, chopped

: 1 small red onion, chopped

: ½ cup (4 ounces) julienned fontina cheese

: ½ cup (4 ounces) julienned prosciutto

**dressing ::**

: 2 tablespoons Dijon mustard

: ½ teaspoon dry mustard

: ⅓ cup red wine vinegar

: ½ cup extra virgin olive oil

: ¼ cup honey

**preparation ::**

Remove any bones, skin, and visible fat from the chicken breasts, and cut them in julienne. In a large skillet, heat 2 tablespoons of the oil over medium-high heat and stir-fry the chicken strips until cooked through and no longer pink, 3 to 4 minutes. Add the garlic and sauté for another minute. Set aside.

In a large bowl, toss the cooked tortellini with the remaining 2 tablespoons olive oil.

To make the dressing, in a medium-sized bowl, combine the Dijon mustard and dry mustard. Whisk in the vinegar until the mustards have dissolved. Then whisk in the oil and honey.

Add the chicken and garlic, bell pepper, celery, red onion, cheese, and prosciutto to the tortellini. Pour the dressing over the mixture and toss gently but thoroughly. Cover with plastic wrap and refrigerate for up to 8 hours, or serve immediately.

# birds ofanother feather salads

For a delicious poultry salad, you need not always start out with a roasted bird, poached breasts, or even leftovers. The deli counters of most super-markets carry a variety of commercially smoked birds, both chicken and turkey. In the dog days of summer, I sometimes use deli turkey for salad. Be sure to ask for the turkey in one or two thick slices so that you can cube it for salad; otherwise the counter person will automatically slice it much too thin. Look for sweet-smelling, ripe melons, and use several vari-eties for color interest, such as honeydew, cantaloupe, and Persian mel-ons. Watermelon tends not to be firm enough. Do not mix the melon balls and the other ingredients together until the last minute, as the melon becomes watery if it stands for any length of time.

# smoked turkey and melon salad with citrus mint vinaigrette

**serves four ::**

: 2 cups cubed smoked turkey (12 ounces)

: 2 cups melon balls from cantaloupe, honeydew, Persian, Crenshaw, or any firm sweet melon

: Salt and freshly ground black pepper

: ½ cup slivered almonds, toasted (page 17)

: Mint sprigs for garnish

**dressing ::**

: 1 tablespoon orange juice concentrate, thawed

: 1 tablespoon chopped fresh mint

: ⅓ cup mayonnaise, homemade (page 16) or high-quality purchased

: ¼ cup sour cream

**preparation ::**

In a large bowl, combine the turkey and melon balls. To make the dressing, in a bowl whisk together the orange juice, mint, may-onnaise, and sour cream. Pour the dressing over the turkey-melon mixture, and toss gently but thoroughly. Season to taste with a pinch of salt and pepper. Turn the salad into a glass serving bowl, sprinkle the almonds over it, and garnish with mint sprigs. Serve immediately, or cover and refrigerate for up to 30 minutes.

94

I first encountered this classic tuna sauce many summers ago in Florence, Italy. It is a northern Italian summer dish, traditionally served on *Ferragosto* or Ascension Day (August 15), according to Pellegrino Arutusi, the nineteenth-century gastronome. It is generally served over cold sliced veal roast. I have substituted a boneless half turkey breast for the veal, and the results are quite delicious. The thin meat slices are arranged overlapping on a large platter and then napped with the piquant sauce and garnished with hard-boiled eggs, paper-thin lemon slices, and capers. The dish should be prepared 24 hours ahead for the flavors to truly blend and permeate the meat. The sauce is also delicious spooned over halved hard-boiled eggs or cold cooked vegetables such as asparagus or green beans. This is a perfect summer dish for entertaining. A crusty bread to mop up the sauce, a crisp green salad of arugula and radicchio, a chilled Soave, and *buon appetito*!

# turkeytonnato

**serves six to eight ::**

: 1 boneless half turkey breast, 3 to 3½ pounds

: 2 cans (7 ounces each) imported Italian tuna packed in olive oil

: 6 flat anchovies, rinsed and dried

: 1½ cups mayonnaise, preferably home-made (see note and page 16) or high-quality purchased

: 2 tablespoons drained capers, plus 1 tablespoon for garnish

: Juice of 1 lemon

: Freshly ground black pepper

: 1 lemon, thinly sliced, for garnish

: 2 hard-boiled eggs, cut into wedges, for garnish

**preparation ::**

Poach the turkey breast according to the master recipe for poaching chicken (page 14), simmering the breast an additional 10 minutes after it comes to the initial boil before letting it cool in the liquid. Poaching is important here, because you want the turkey to be as moist as possible. When it is cool enough to handle, remove any skin and slice the meat as thinly as possible. Set the slices aside while you prepare the sauce.

In a food processor or blender, place the tuna with its oil, the anchovies, mayonnaise, and 2 tablespoons of the capers. Process or blend until the mixture is smooth and creamy, 2 to 3 minutes. Taste and season with lemon juice and pepper. Since the anchovies and capers are salty, additional salt may not be required.

Spread a little of the sauce over the bottom of the platter. Arrange a layer of turkey on the platter, slightly overlapping, and then coat with a layer of sauce. Continue in this fashion until you have just enough of the sauce to coat the top layer. There will be 2 or 3 layers. Cover tightly with plastic wrap and refrigerate for at least 24 hours. When ready to serve, remove the wrap, scraping any excess sauce off the plastic and spreading it over the turkey. Then garnish the platter with the lemon slices, egg wedges, and remaining tablespoon of capers.

Serve at once.

**note ::** *I made the tuna sauce with domestic tuna and purchased mayonnaise, and discovered it does not have the depth of flavor that is obtained by using the imported tuna and home-made mayonnaise. Don't be tempted to take a shortcut here. This is one recipe that really benefits from using homemade mayonnaise. Use half extra virgin olive oil and half vegetable oil in your preparation.*

This recipe comes from my friend and assistant Liz Lapham. For years she has been creative in turning her husband Bev's hunting bounty into delicious dishes. One summer day her freezer offered up some pheasant breasts, which she transformed into this salad. It combines the flavor of poached pheasant with the piquancy of tarragon and the snap of lemon mayonnaise. When preparing this salad, be sure to leave enough time for it to gel completely.

# jellied pheasant and tarragon salad

**preparation ::**

In a large saucepan, heat to boiling the stock, tarragon, and onion and lemon slices. Lower the heat to a simmer, season the pheasant breasts with salt and white pepper, and place them in the simmering broth. Simmer the breasts for approximately 25 minutes. Check for doneness by cutting into the breasts. Remove the meat from the bones and discard the skin. Cut the meat into ½-inch cubes. Refrigerate, covered, until ready to assemble.

Chill the stock in the refrigerator and then remove and discard any surface fat with a slotted spoon.

In a large bowl, toss the meat gently with the parsley, peas, and mushrooms. Spray a 6-cup ring mold with nonstick cooking spray. Arrange the pheasant mixture in the mold. Strain and heat the stock. Pour the Madeira into a small bowl and sprinkle the gelatin over it. When the gelatin has dissolved, pour the Madeira mixture into the heated stock and stir to combine. Pour the stock gently over the pheasant mixture in the ring mold.

Cover with plastic wrap and chill until firm, 3 to 4 hours.

To make the lemon mayonnaise, stir the lemon juice and grated zest into the mayonnaise.

When ready to serve, unmold the salad on a platter lined with greens. (See the note on unmolding Chicken and Cranberries with Green Pea Mousse, page 47.) Place a small bowl of the lemon mayonnaise in the center of the mold.

**serves six ::**

: 3½ cups chicken stock, homemade (page 19) or high-quality purchased

: ¼ cup chopped fresh tarragon, or 2 teaspoons dried tarragon

: 1 slice yellow onion

: 1 slice lemon

: 3 whole pheasant breasts, about 8 ounces each

: Salt and freshly ground white pepper

: 3 tablespoons minced parsley

: 1 cup cooked petite peas

: 1 jar (about 7 ounces) button mushrooms, drained

: ½ cup Madeira

: 2 packets (¼ ounce each) unflavored gelatin

: Greens of your choice for serving

**lemon mayonnaise ::**

: 2 tablespoons fresh lemon juice

: 2 teaspoons grated lemon zest

: 1 cup mayonnaise, homemade (page 16) or high-quality purchased

97

Quail are enjoyed in many parts of this country and in Europe as well. Recently when in Italy, I was surprised to see quail in the local supermarket, tidily tucked in their plastic wrap, all cleaned and ready to go. I purchased some and, since it was warm weather, decided to grill them. The end result was a delicious warm salad for two. The salad was accompanied by chunks of Tuscan bread to mop up the savory juices, and a glass of robust Chianti. With the moon rising over the shapes of the cypress trees, *perfetto*!

# grilledquailsalad

**serves two (two quail per person) ::**

: 4 quail, cleaned (or 1 Rock Cornish game hen)

: Melted butter for brushing

: Salt and freshly ground black pepper

: ½ cup red wine

: 4 cups loosely packed baby arugula or mix of field greens

**dressing ::**

: 2 tablespoons balsamic vinegar, plus more for drizzling

: Pinch of salt

: Dash of freshly ground black pepper

: ⅓ cup extra virgin olive oil

**preparation ::**

Prepare a charcoal fire or gas grill (or preheat the broiler). Split the quail open along the backbone and flatten them slightly with a cleaver, breast side down.

Brush both sides of the quail with melted butter, and sprinkle with salt and pepper. Grill the quail, breast side down, for 15 to 20 minutes, or until browned, turning them once. Baste 2 or 3 times with spoonfuls of red wine. Pierce the quail with the tip of a knife. If the juices run clear, they are done.

To make the dressing, add the vinegar to a small bowl, and dissolve the salt in the vinegar. Add the pepper, and whisk in the olive oil.

Arrange the greens on a serving platter, or divide them between 2 individual plates.

When the quail are done, place them on top of the greens. Drizzle the dressing over them and serve at once.

# roasted duck and fennel salad with balsamic vinaigrette

**serves four to six ::**

: 1½ pounds boneless
  duck breasts (see note)

: ⅓ cup Marsala

: ⅓ cup orange juice

: ¾ cup extra virgin
  olive oil, divided

: 6 tablespoons balsamic
  vinegar, divided

: 2 bulbs fennel, chopped

: Juice of ½ lemon
  (about 3 tablespoons)

: 2 large navel oranges,
  peeled and sectioned,
  white pith removed

: Salt and freshly
  ground black pepper

: ½ cup oil-cured black
  olives, pits removed

Due to the high fat content of the domesticated Pekin (Long Island) duck widely available in the supermarket, a 4½-pound duck serves only 2 or 3 duck aficionados at the most. Duck breasts alone are generally available and are most suitable for this salad. I like to serve this in the winter months as an elegant first course or for a luncheon. The marinating tenderizes the duck and helps prevent it from drying out during the cooking process. A crusty loaf of bread, perhaps with fennel seeds, and a bottle of robust red wine complete the festive menu.

**preparation ::**

Lay the breast halves skin side down on your work surface and trim any protruding fat.

Turn them over and score the skin side with a sharp knife, cutting not quite through to the flesh. Set aside while you make the marinade.

In a small bowl, mix together the Marsala, orange juice, ¼ cup of the olive oil, and 3 tablespoons of the balsamic vinegar. Pour the mixture into a flat dish, and place the duck breasts, skin side down, in the marinade.

Cover with plastic wrap and refrigerate overnight. Turn the breasts several times.

The next day, preheat the oven to 450°F. Line a baking sheet with foil. Lay the duck breasts skin-side up on the baking sheet, and roast for 20 minutes for rare meat (155°F), 10 minutes longer if you prefer the meat well done. If you are using smaller breasts, check them after 12 minutes. Remove from the oven. The temperature will be about 160°F after

having rested for a few minutes. The duck may be prepared and refrigerated, covered, up to a day ahead.

Wash the fennel bulbs and cut off the tops where they meet the bulb. Split the bulbs and remove the core. Dice the fennel into ¼-inch cubes. Sprinkle with the lemon juice and place in a bowl. Dice the orange sections into ½-inch cubes and add to the fennel.

To make the dressing, whisk the remaining 3 tablespoons balsamic vinegar with salt and pepper to taste, and then whisk in the remaining ½ cup olive oil. Reserve ¼ cup.

When ready to serve, arrange the fennel-orange mixture on a platter and pour the dressing over it. Slice the breasts on the diagonal, removing any excess fat, and lay the duck slices, overlapping slightly, over the fennel-orange mixture. Strew the olives over all, and drizzle with the remaining ¼ cup dressing. Serve at once.

**note ::** *The Pekin duck breasts average about 6 ounces per half, while the Magret breasts, from the ducks raised to produce foie gras, run between 10 and 12 ounces per half breast.*

If you have been part of the fried turkey trend, you know how good a bird deep-fried in oil can be. For the past two years, we have made it part of our holiday celebrations. I do believe it is a guy thing. Men love standing around the bubbling pot, watching the turkey fry while the temperature hovers in the teens. After the feasting, there is always enough turkey left to make a salad, soup, or casserole. Here's the way my leftover turkey ended up on a New Year's Day buffet. It was lifted to another level when served in a shimmering ruby ring of cranberry. Make the ring six to eight hours before serving, to allow time for it to set.

# newyear'sturkeysalad inacranberryring

**serves six to eight ::**

**cranberry ring ::**
: 1 cup orange juice
: 1 cup water
: 2 packets (¼ ounce each) unflavored gelatin
: ¼ teaspoon salt
: 1 cup cranberry juice cocktail
: 1 can (16 ounces) whole cranberry sauce, or 2 cups leftover home-made cranberry sauce

**turkey salad ::**
: 3 cups cubed leftover roast or fried turkey, both white and dark meat, skin removed
: 1 cup diced celery
: 1 large sweet potato, baked or microwaved, cubed
: ½ cup chopped pecans, toasted (page 17)
: ½ cup dried cranberries

: Finely chopped parsley for garnish

**dressing ::**
: 1 tablespoon fresh lemon juice
: Salt and freshly ground black pepper
: ¾ cup mayonnaise, homemade (page 16) or high-quality purchased

**preparation ::**

To make the cranberry ring, in a saucepan, bring the orange juice and the water to a boil. Add the gelatin and salt; stir until the gelatin dissolves. Stir in the cranberry juice. Chill until partially set, about 1 hour. Stir in the cranberry sauce. Spray a 6-cup ring mold with nonstick cooking spray. Pour the mixture into the mold and chill for 6 to 8 hours or overnight.

To make the salad, place the turkey in a mixing bowl; add the celery, sweet potato, pecans, and dried cranberries.

To make the dressing, in a small bowl, whisk the lemon juice with salt and pepper to taste. Whisk in the mayonnaise and then pour the dressing over the turkey mixture. Toss gently but thoroughly. Cover and refrigerate for up to 8 hours.

When ready to serve, unmold the cranberry ring on a large platter, and mound the turkey salad in the center. (See the note on unmolding Chicken and Cranberries with Green Pea Mousse, page 47). Dust with parsley and serve.

103

I first tasted this salad when I worked in the old Statler Hotel building in Boston. The dish, which was served in the hotel restaurant, was wildly popular and was reputed to be a deep secret. I managed to extract the recipe from a hotel employee, but it was written in such huge quantities that it was difficult to scale it down for two or even six people. I thought because of the name of the salad that Maurice must be part of the hotel's kitchen staff. I later learned that the Netherland Plaza Hotel in Cincinnati also served a Maurice salad, as did Hudson's department stores in Michigan! The only real difference seemed to be in the choice of chicken or turkey. Each claimed it was a secret recipe. Maurice certainly got around. I've done my best to re-create a fond memory here, with the tip of a toque to Maurice, wherever you are.

# thesecretmauricesalad

**serves six to eight ::**

- 1 whole chicken breast (or about 2 cups julienned cooked chicken), or ½ pound deli turkey, julienned
- ½ pound boiled ham, julienned
- ½ pound thinly sliced Swiss cheese, julienned
- ½ cup thinly sliced sweet gherkins, or ¼ cup drained sweet pickle relish
- 1 small head iceberg lettuce, shredded
- ¼ cup chopped chives for garnish
- 3 medium tomatoes, cut into quarters, for garnish

**dressing ::**

- 1½ cups mayonnaise, homemade (page 16) or high-quality purchased
- 2 teaspoons white wine vinegar
- 2 tablespoons grated onion
- 1½ teaspoons Worcestershire sauce
- 2 tablespoons finely chopped parsley
- 2 hard-boiled eggs, peeled and grated
- Salt and freshly ground black pepper

**preparation ::**

If you are using uncooked chicken, poach it according to the master recipe for poaching chicken (page 14). When it is cool enough to handle, remove any bones, skin, and visible fat, and cut it into ¼-inch julienne. Place the chicken or turkey in a large bowl, along with the ham, cheese, pickles, and lettuce.

To make the dressing, in a medium bowl, whisk together the mayonnaise, vinegar, grated onion, and Worcestershire sauce. Fold in the parsley and grated egg. Add salt and pepper to taste. (You may prepare the dressing several hours ahead and refrigerate it until ready to serve.)

Pour the dressing over the chicken or turkey mixture, tossing gently but thoroughly. Divide into portions and mound each portion on a plate. Sprinkle each plate with chopped chives and garnish with 2 wedges of tomato. Serve immediately.

# index

107

# tableofequivalents

The exact equivalents in the following tables have been rounded for convenience.

## liquid/dry measures

| u.s. | metric |
|------|--------|
| ¼ teaspoon | 1.25 milliliters |
| ½ teaspoon | 2.5 milliliters |
| 1 teaspoon | 5 milliliters |
| 1 tablespoon (*3 teaspoons*) | 15 milliliters |
| 1 fluid ounce (*2 tablespoons*) | 30 milliliters |
| ¼ cup | 60 milliliters |
| ⅓ cup | 80 milliliters |
| ½ cup | 120 milliliters |
| 1 cup | 240 milliliters |
| 1 pint (2 cups) | 480 milliliters |
| 1 quart (*4 cups, 32 ounces*) | 960 milliliters |
| 1 gallon (*4 quarts*) | 3.84 liters |
| 1 ounce (*by weight*) | 28 grams |
| 1 pound | 454 grams |
| 2.2 pounds | 1 kilogram |

## length

| u.s. | metric |
|------|--------|
| ⅛ inch | 3 millimeters |
| ¼ inch | 6 millimeters |
| ½ inch | 12 millimeters |
| 1 inch | 2.5 centimeters |

## oven temperature

| fahrenheit | celsius | gas |
|------------|---------|-----|
| 250 | 120 | ½ |
| 275 | 140 | 1 |
| 300 | 150 | 2 |
| 325 | 160 | 3 |
| 350 | 180 | 4 |
| 375 | 190 | 5 |
| 400 | 200 | 6 |
| 425 | 220 | 7 |
| 450 | 230 | 8 |
| 475 | 240 | 9 |
| 500 | 260 | 10 |

108

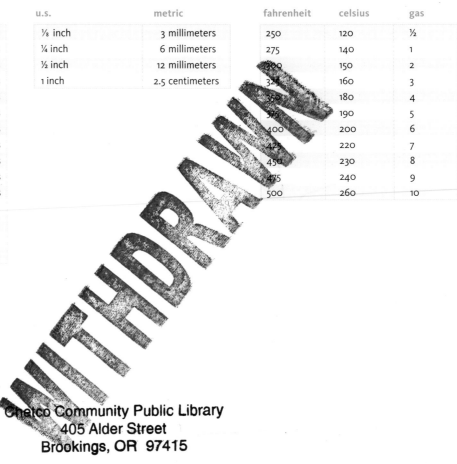